# Lee Kong Chian

Educationalist

Entrepreneur Philanthropist

# Lee Kong Chian
## Educationalist Entrepreneur Philanthropist

**Kenneth Lyen**
*Rainbow Centre, Singapore*

World Scientific

NEW JERSEY • LONDON • SINGAPORE • BEIJING • SHANGHAI • HONG KONG • TAIPEI • CHENNAI • TOKYO

*Published by*

World Scientific Publishing Co. Pte. Ltd.
5 Toh Tuck Link, Singapore 596224
*USA office:* 27 Warren Street, Suite 401-402, Hackensack, NJ 07601
*UK office:* 57 Shelton Street, Covent Garden, London WC2H 9HE

Library of Congress Control Number: 2024934144

**British Library Cataloguing-in-Publication Data**
A catalogue record for this book is available from the British Library.

**LEE KONG CHIAN**
**Educationalist Entrepreneur Philanthropist**



ISBN 978-981-12-8521-9 (hardcover)
ISBN 978-981-12-8559-2 (paperback)
ISBN 978-981-12-8522-6 (ebook for institutions)
ISBN 978-981-12-8523-3 (ebook for individuals)

For any available supplementary material, please visit
https://www.worldscientific.com/worldscibooks/10.1142/13648#t=suppl

Typeset by Stallion Press
Email: enquiries@stallionpress.com

# Foreword

Singapore needs heroes. I regard Lee Kong Chian as a hero of Singapore. I am therefore very pleased that Dr. Kenneth Lyon has written a biography of the great but humble man. I regard him as a hero for the following reasons.

First, I admire the fact that, by hard work, ability, and good luck, he rose from poverty to great prosperity. He made his fortune in rubber and in banking. He made Lee Rubber and OCBC Bank two of the most successful companies in Singapore.

Second, I admire his philanthropy. He started the Lee Foundation and endowed it generously. When he died he left half his estate to the foundation. The Lee Foundation is the most important foundation in Singapore. It has benefited education, science, research, health, welfare, culture and the arts and many other good causes. It has given scholarships to thousands of students and helped them to fulfill their dream of a university education.

Third, I admire him because of his character and the Confucian values he championed. In spite of his great wealth, he was humble and approachable. He was honest and honourable. He lived a simple and frugal life. He was filial to his father and father-in-law. He was faithful to his wife. He was a good father to his six children. He treated his friends, employees and everyone else with respect and kindness. He could speak Chinese, English, Malay and Tamil. He believed in racial equality and in building an inclusive society.

Malcolm MacDonald, the then British High Commissioner in Southeast Asia wrote this about Lee Kong Chian: "Dato Lee has remained utterly unspoilt, humble and unassuming in spite of the extraordinary influence that he can exercise in commerce, finance and politics. His humanity is one of the masks of his true greatness."

Tommy Koh<br>
Founding Chairman<br>
Lee Kong Chian Natural History Museum<br>
National University of Singapore

# Preface

Lee Kong Chian (1893–1967) is one of Singapore's most outstanding figures in the history of Singapore and Southeast Asia. His contributions have had a lasting impact on the region.

Although he came from a poor family background, Lee Kong Chian had the good fortune to meet Tan Kah Kee, a pioneering businessman and philanthropist, who helped Kong Chian to become a highly successful entrepreneur and to co-found the Oversea-Chinese Banking Corporation. Lee Kong Chian played a key role in the development of the region's economy, and his contributions helped to create jobs and stimulate growth. He became one of the richest man in Southeast Asia in the 1950s to 1960s, and yet he lived a simple frugal lifestyle.

Lee Kong Chian was a generous philanthropist who donated millions of dollars to charitable causes throughout his life. He used his personal money to start the Lee Foundation, which continues to donate to educational institutions, healthcare, and social welfare.

My purpose of writing this book is to pay homage and to thank Lee Kong Chian and the Lee Foundation for supporting the organisations and schools that I was a member of the board of governors. These included the Movement for the Intellectually Disabled of Singapore (MINDS), the Rainbow Centre, and the Anglo-Chinese School. Quite a number of my students applied to and were admitted to the Lee Kong Chian School of Medicine, and they continue to help many patients and their families. This book is written from the perspective of the innumerable recipients of Lee Kong Chian and the Lee Foundation's generosity, rather than from an academic historian's analysis.

The book is the first extensive account of this distinguished individual, following him from childhood to his passing. He leaves behind a remarkable legacy, which will continue to impact the lives of countless numbers of people in Singapore and beyond.

Kenneth Lyen

# About the Author

Dr. Kenneth Lyen is a paediatrician, writer, composer, and is involved in special education.

He graduated from Oxford University Medical School before undertaking specialist paediatric training at the Great Ormond Street Hospital for Children in London and the Children's Hospital of Philadelphia. Upon his return to Singapore, he was appointed senior lecturer and consultant at the National University of Singapore.

Outside of clinical work, he has been involved in special education. He was on the board of management of the Movement for the Intellectually Disabled of Singapore (MINDS), which held its meetings at the Lee Kong Chian Gardens School. He also founded three schools under the Rainbow Centre, which helps disabled and autistic children, namely, the Rainbow Centre at Margaret Drive (1987), Yishun Park (1995), and Woodlands (2018). He is grateful to the Lee Foundation for supporting these special schools. For his work with disabled children, Dr. Lyen received the Public Service Medal in 1997 and the Public Service Star in 2022.

Dr. Lyen has co-authored 16 books on a variety of topics, including paediatrics, parenting, creativity, education, and musical theatre. He has published original research papers on paediatric endocrinology, neurology, and infectious diseases and medical review articles. He has previously served on the editorial board of the *Singapore Medical Journal*, *Motherhood* and *Young Families*. He has composed music for 33 musicals that have been staged in Singapore.

# Dedications

This book is dedicated to:

My wife, Dr. Huang Yuen Chin

My son, Dr. Stephen Lyen, his wife, Dr. Claudia Hon, and their children, Max and Chloe

My daughter, Janice Claire Lyen, her husband, Benjamin Phipps, and their children, Elizabeth, Joseph, Jude and Christopher

My sons, Paul and Brian

They have all supported me in writing this book.

# Acknowledgements

Many thanks to Professor Tommy Koh for writing the Foreword and to Mary Ng En Tzu for translating several Chinese texts and proofreading the book.

I would also like to thank the following for their support in writing this book and for granting me permission to publish their pictures and photographs:

Julian Wang
Kelvin Koh Chi Wee
Irene Tan Ai Poh
Chia Chor Yann
Sophie Lim Pey Pey
Ho Li Yan
Eric Tan Ee
Cheryl Lim
Tan Eng Luan
Dr. Fong Kah Leng

I thank members of Lee Kong Chian's family for providing the photographs and for allowing me to use them. My sincere thanks also goes to Ms. Yugarani Thanabalasingam from World Scientific Publishing, who supported me at every step of this journey with trust, patience and efficiency.

There are many others whose names are not listed above, but have been indispensable in the writing of this book, to whom I am extremely grateful.

# Contents

# 1 Early Life

## Furong Village, Nan'an County

Lee Kong Chian (李光前, *Lǐ Guāngqián*) was born on 18 October 1893 in Furong Village (芙蓉) in Nan'an County (南安), Fujian (福建), China, towards the end of the Qing (清, Manchu) Dynasty. His father, Lee Kuo Chuan (李国专, *Lǐ Guózhuān*), was a schoolteacher who had to supplement his meagre income by working as a tailor and a hairdresser outside of school hours. He started a small inn in Xiamen (厦门), but business was so bad that he had to close it down. Lee Kong Chian was sent to a traditional Chinese school in his hometown, but to supplement his school fees, he had to herd cattle, which he did with bare feet. His mother had passed away when he was only 8 years old.[1]

## Sea Journey to Singapore (1903)

At the turn of the century, China was in turmoil, and there was nationwide economic hardship. In 1903, when Lee Kong Chian was 10 years old, his father decided to find work in Singapore, which was a prosperous British colony, leaving him behind. Very shortly after, he followed his father to Singapore.

## The Blanket Story

Lee Kong Chian was only 10 years old when he travelled to Singapore. Coincidentally, travelling on the same ship was Tan Kah Kee (陳嘉庚), who was already a rich businessman. The weather was freezing cold, and Tan

Kah Kee offered a blanket to passengers whose surnames were Tan. Many of these passengers, out of desperation, pretended that their surnames were Tan in order to collect a blanket. But when Tan Kah Kee walked around the ship, he noticed a boy shivering and asked him why he had not collected a blanket; the boy replied that his surname was Lee, not Tan, and was therefore not eligible for the blanket. His honest reply impressed Tan Kah Kee, who then announced that everybody would get a blanket. Tan Kah Kee later learnt that the boy's name was Lee Kong Chian. He gave the boy his name card, asking the youngster to contact him when he arrived in Singapore. They were to meet again several years later.[1]

## Anglo-Tamil School, Singapore (1904–1909)

In Singapore, Lee Kuo Chuan and his son Kong Chian lived above a shophouse belonging to Lim Loh (林露 or 林路), who was also from Nan'an County and the father of Lim Bo Seng (林谋盛), a martyr who would be killed by the Japanese during the Second World War.

Lee Kuo Chuan made a living as a tailor, while Kong Chian initially attended Yangzheng School (养正学堂). Although Kong Chian had good exam scores and would have gained admission to the more prestigious Anglo-Chinese School, the tuition fees were rather high and mostly only children of wealthy businessmen could afford to attend this school. His father could not pay such high school fees and so sent him to the cheaper Anglo-Tamil School along Serangoon Road, where the school fees was 25 cents per month. He learnt English and Tamil at this school but in the afternoons and weekends, his father would send him to continue learning Chinese at another school, the Chong Cheng School (崇正学校) located at Aliwal Street. Subsequently, Kong Chian switched to Tao Nan School (道南学校) and St. Joseph's Institution.

The students at the Anglo-Tamil School were predominantly from Sri Lanka and South India. Most came from poor families and could not afford to buy shoes and so went to school barefoot. Many of them earned extra money by herding cattle and milking cows. As Lee Kong Chian had lived in the countryside of Nan'an County, he was accustomed to walking barefooted, and as he was also experienced in looking after cattle, he got along well with his schoolmates, and they became good friends. These Indian students usually communicated in Tamil, and although Lee Kong

Chian initially did not understand the language, he soon learned to speak Tamil after making friends with them. The standard of English teaching was reputed to be quite high at this school, and being diligent, Lee Kong Chian soon laid for himself a solid foundation in English.

## Scholarship for Nanjing's Jinan School, China (1909–1910)

The Qing Dynasty was the last of the imperial dynasties in China. By the late 19$^{th}$ and early 20$^{th}$ century, it was becoming increasingly unpopular, especially after its defeat in the Opium Wars (1839–1842 and 1856–1860), followed by several uprisings, including the Taiping Rebellion (1850–1864), the Dungan Revolt (1862–1877), and the Boxer Uprising (1899–1901). In 1895, China suffered a humiliating defeat in the first Sino-Japanese War. These losses and uprisings failed to topple the Qing Dynasty, but there were many rebels, including Sun Yat Sen (孙逸仙), who had started to recruit dissidents to overthrow the Qing Dynasty.[2,3]

To counter the influence of Sun Yat Sen, the Qing government decided to introduce the Huairou Policy (怀柔政策), where they awarded scholarships to the children of overseas Chinese to study back home in China. In 1908, the Qing government sent an official, Wang Sixue（汪视学), to Singapore and, together with the recommendation of the Chinese Chamber of Commerce & Industry Committee, they recruited Lee Kong Chian and more than 40 other Chinese teenagers to study in Nanjing's Jinan (暨南) School. Around that time some millions of Chinese had left China to find work overseas but they still maintained sentimental links with their homeland. This trans-regional framework allowed for fluidity of movements, especially with regard to returning for education back in China.[4] In 1909, at the age of 15, Lee Kong Chian returned to China to start schooling. He was a brilliant student, excelling in mathematics, physics and chemistry, and two years later, he graduated first in his class.

## Lee Kong Chian and the Meridian Time Lines (1910)

One of Lee Kong Chian's classmates was Tan Ee Leong (陈维龙, *Chen Weilong*), who he met in 1910. In his memoirs, Weilong wrote about an incident when their teacher was explaining to them the Earth's theoretical meridian lines: when travelling from the west to the east, the distance between two meridian lines would advance time by 4 minutes; conversely, time would be dialled back by 4 minutes when travelling back from the east to the west. Weilong and his classmates could not understand the concept, but it was only when he consulted Lee Kong Chian that it was explained to him with crystal clarity.

In addition to excelling in mathematics and science, Lee Kong Chian was also a good writer. In his school, the best essays were selected by the teacher and used as examples for teaching junior students. However, there were two other classmates whose essays were used more frequently, but one of the Jinan School students remembered that some of Lee Kong Chian's essays were also selected for teaching.

After graduating from Jinan School in the spring of 1911 as the top student, 18-year-old Lee Kong Chian went on to Beijing Tsinghua High School (清华附中) for two years, the equivalent of the current sixth form pre-university school. Then, he enrolled in Tsinghua College (清华大学) in Beijing for further studies, but soon transferred to Tangshan College of Railway and Mining (唐山铁道矿业学院), the predecessor of Southwest Jiaotong University (西南交通大学).[5] This school had been set up to train professionals in mining and building roads and railways, and it was considered one of the top colleges in China and some of the teachers were from England and Scotland. Lee Kong Chian studied civil engineering, but unfortunate political events in 1911 stopped his studies.

## The Xinhai Revolution (辛亥革命, 1911)

The revolution that finally led to the ultimate end of the Qing Dynasty started in 1911 and was led by several anti-Qing revolutionaries, including Sun Yat Sen. While studying at the Tangshan College of Railway and Mining, Lee Kong Chian joined the Tongmenghui (同盟會, Revolutionary Alliance) that was the antecedent to the Kuomintang (國民黨). This was a hothouse of revolutionary fomentation. To show his support for Sun Yat Sen, Lee Kong

Chian cut off his queue (or pigtail hair). However, to avoid running afoul of the authorities, he donned a wig.

## Yuan Shikai and the Closure of Tangshan College of Railway and Mining (1912)

Yuan Shikai (袁世凯) was an army commander who rapidly rose through the ranks and helped overthrow the Qing Dynasty, forcing the abdication of the boy emperor Puyi. He took over the presidency of China from Sun Yat Sen in 1912, who had earlier served as the first provisional president of the Republic of China. However, to consolidate his position, he started to arrest the supporters of Sun Yat Sen and closed down several organisations and institutions, including the Tangshan College of Railway and Mining, where Lee Kong Chian was studying.

## Return to Singapore (1912)

The college closure meant that Lee Kong Chian's ambition to become an engineer was unachievable, so he left China and returned to Singapore in 1912 at the age of 19. One of the passengers on the boat, Zhang Fuying (张福英), described Kong Chian as "unsociable but down-to-earth". After spending four years in China, Kong Chian had learnt western ideologies and science, but he had also experienced the violence and turmoil in China's political landscape. He decided that Singapore was the place to pursue his dreams.[6,7]

## Teaching and Other Jobs

When Lee Kong Chian went to China on a scholarship, his father also moved back to his hometown. However, when he decided to return to Singapore in 1912, his father stayed on in China.

Upon returning to Singapore in 1912, Lee Kong Chian initially took up teaching despite the relatively low salary. He taught at his alma mater,

Chong Cheng School, in the daytime and Tao Nan School at night. Sometimes, he would spend the night in the classroom, joining up a couple of tables to form a makeshift bed.

## Mosquitoes

As Lee Kong Chian was fluent in both Chinese and English, he found an extra job working as a telecom interpreter for *Lat Pau* (叻报, Le Bao), a Singapore Chinese newspaper. At that time, Chinese newsrooms were poorly managed and were short of capital to buy various telecom-transmitted news. In contrast, English language newspapers like *The Straits Times*, with better communication, were able to access international news. Therefore, most foreign news were translated from English into Chinese. Lee Kong Chian would often bring home that day's English newspaper to be translated at night, and he often worked past midnight. In those days, electric lights were not common, and Lee Kong Chian's sleeping quarters did not have an electric light, so he lit candles; and while writing with his right hand, he would swipe away mosquitoes with his left. Once, a fellow teacher recounted that when he saw the mosquito bites on Lee Kong Chian, he asked him if he was afraid of catching mosquito-borne diseases. Lee Kong Chian's reply was to quote an ancient saying: "If you don't work hard when young, it's useless regretting it when you are old". Then, Lee Kong Chian explained that he had been bitten by mosquitoes all his life, and he was no longer afraid of them. The teacher could only shake his head and walk away with a wry smile.

## Study Courses (1912–1914)

Lee Kong Chian still strongly aspired to be an engineer, so he changed jobs and became an assistant field surveyor with the British colonial government's Public Works Department (PWD). As part of the training, he had to take a special survey and geodesy mathematics course organised by the PWD, but this bonded him for five years. In addition, Lee Kong Chian decided to go further and embarked on a correspondence course in civil engineering offered by an American university.

The work was gruelling, and Lee Kong Chian had to wake up at 5 am every day in order to start work at 6 am. There was a demand for engineers because of the rapidly expanding tin mining and rubber plantation activities in Malaya, which resulted in the creation of new towns and roads. Engineers were required to conduct land surveys, develop mines, determine where best to grow rubber trees, and advise where to construct roads and railway transport. As part of the training programme, Lee Kong Chian travelled to Malaya, where he had to climb mountains, wade rivers to measure their depth, map out the geology of the region, and determine where to lay new roads. All this was carried out in the hot sun and also stormy weather. At night, he had to draw survey maps to be assessed by his supervisors.

In 1914, at the age of 21, he graduated from the survey and geodesy course as well as the correspondence university course in civil engineering.

## China Domestic Goods (Guohuo) Company (中华国货公司)

Quite by chance, Lee Kong Chian happened to meet a Chinese community leader named Cheng Hee Chuan (庄希泉, Zhuang Xiquan), who was working for a private business, the China Domestic Goods Company. Cheng Hee Chuan was very impressed by Lee Kong Chian's intelligence and offered him a job in his company and even offered to pay off the remainder of his 5-year government bond. Realising that his chances of promotion in a British-run government company was limited, Lee Kong Chian decided to accept Cheng Hee Chuan's offer in 1915. He was then asked to manage the import of goods from China to Singapore, which was re-exported to Europe. The First World War had started in 1914 and had caused a shortage of European merchandise. Unfortunately, the quality of the products from China was inferior, and this venture failed.

The head of the China Domestic Goods Company happened to be Tan Kah Kee, whom Lee Kong Chian had met 11 years earlier on board the ship to Singapore. The two of them were destined to meet again in 1916, and this would change both their lives.

## References


1. Li, Y. R. 李远荣. (1998) *The Memoirs of Lee Kong Chian.* 《李光前传》 香港: 名流出版社. (Call no.: Chinese RSING 959.57 LYR-[HIS])
2. Nor-Afidah Abd Rahman and Wee, J. Lee Kong Chian, *Singapore Infopedia.* https://eresources.nlb.gov.sg/infopedia/articles/SIP_978_2006-06-16.html
3. Wikipedia. Lee Kong Chian, https://en.wikipedia.org/wiki/Lee_Kong_Chian
4. Seah, L. (2008) Jinan University, Lee Kong Chian, and the Nanyang Connection 1900–1942. BiblioAsia, Volume 4, Issue 1, pp. 26–37.
5. Li, Z., editor (2006) *Lee Kong Chian: A Model of Overseas Chinese.* Guang Da Publisher Ltd Co.
6. Zheng, B. S. (1997) *The Memoirs of Lee Kong Chian.* 郑炳山. 《李光前传》 北京: 中国华侨出版社, p. 18. (Call no.: Chinese RSING 959.57 ZBS-[HIS]).
7. Visscher, S. (2007) *The Business of Politics and Ethnicity: A History of the Singapore Chinese Chamber of Commerce and Industry.* Singapore: NUS Press, p. 48. (Call no.: RSING 381.0605957 VIS)

# 2 Career and Life Decisions

## Tan Kah Kee (陳嘉庚, 1874–1961)

Tan Kah Kee

*Source*: Wikipedia.

Tan Kah Kee was a prominent Chinese Hokkien businessman and philanthropist. Born in Jimei in the Fujian province, he came to Singapore at the age of 16 to work for his father, a businessman running a rice company and a pineapple plantation. However, his father's business fell into debt, and Kah Kee had to close the company down in 1903. Tan Kah Kee then started his own business, the China Domestic Goods (Guohuo) Company (中华国货公司), which was involved in rubber plantations, rice fields, shipping, a biscuit factory, and the manufacture of products such as tyres and shoes. He was so successful that his business was at its prime between 1912 and 1914. By coincidence, he first met the 10-year-old Lee Kong Chian in 1903 when they were both onboard the same ship travelling to Singapore. Thirteen years later, in 1916, he bumped into the 22-year-old Lee Kong Chian, who had started working in his Guohuo company a year before. Tan Kah Kee's manager, Cheng Hee Chuan, had earlier persuaded Lee Kong Chian to leave the British colonial government's Public Works Department and even bought off his 5-year bond.[1,2]

## The Umbrella (1916)

Sitting at a hawker street food stall, Lee Kong Chian was having his dinner when he noticed someone rushing out carrying a packet of food, trying to avoid the heavy rain. He immediately recognised the person was Tan Kah Kee, the head owner of the company he was working for. So, he ran after him and offered his umbrella. Being an impatient man, Kah Kee took the umbrella but passed Kong Chian his name card and asked him to go to his office the next day to collect back his umbrella.[3]

The following day, Lee Kong Chian went to Tan Kah Kee's company office to retrieve his umbrella. He was warmly welcomed and given a cup of tea. Kong Chian reminded Kah Kee that they had been on the same boat sailing to Singapore in the freezing winter of 1903. It was only then that Kah Kee realised Kong Chian had been the boy who had refused to take his blanket because he had only offered them to passengers whose surnames were "Tan", and he remembered how impressed he had been by the boy's honesty.

As they continued their conversation, there was a sudden commotion outside the office. A staff member interrupted them, saying that there was a foreigner outside who wanted something, but as none of them understood English, the man wanted to speak to the manager, but was not allowed in. The man then became angry and started shouting. Tan Kah Kee and Lee Kong Chian hurried out to try to placate the foreigner. As soon as the foreigner saw Tan Kah Kee, he knew Kah Kee was the boss, and he began to explain why he was in their office. However, even Kah Kee could not understand English, and was beginning to feel embarrassed. Then, Lee Kong Chian calmly stepped forward and starting speaking to the Westerner, who began to vigorously nod his head in agreement. Kong Chian then explained to Kah Kee that the gentleman was an American businessman who wanted to find out how he could purchase rubber from their company and the procedure to follow.

## The American Businessman

Tan Kah Kee had long been interested in the direct trading of rubber with non-British businessmen because he wanted to bypass the British who had monopolised the ownership and trading of rubber; they also controlled the price of rubber. Singapore and Malayan rubber had to go through British agents who channelled the rubber sales to the European market for companies such as Guthrie, Sime Darby, Boustead and the Harrison Group. American businessmen, on the other hand, were dissatisfied with the profits taken by British banks and the obstacles they created; hence, they had come to Singapore to open their own branch to buy rubber directly from businessmen in Malaya and Singapore.

So, when this American businessman turned up to purchase rubber, Tan Kah Kee was elated, but he realised that none of his company staff could speak adequate English. On observing that Lee Kong Chian was displaying a strong command of English, Kah Kee immediately wanted to recruit him into his rubber company, the Khiam Aik (Qianyi) Company (谦益公司), to help export rubber overseas, especially to America and also develop the non-British and non-European market.

## No Disloyalty

Tan Kah Kee asked his manager Cheng Hee Chuan to convey the message to Lee Kong Chian that he wanted Kong Chian to be transferred from the Chinese Domestic Goods Company to another branch of his company, the Khiam Aik Company, which dealt predominantly with the export of rubber from Malaya. To Cheng Hee Chuan's surprise, Lee Kong Chian flatly turned down the offer, giving the reason that since it had been Cheng Hee Chuan who had talent-scouted him, offered him his current job, and also paid off his government bond, it would therefore be disloyal to "job hop" without fully paying back the largesse that had been given to him. Cheng Hee Chuan tried to persuade Kong Chian to accept the offer, saying that Tan Kah Kee was his close friend and both companies belonged to Kah Kee.

Cheng Hee Chuan also offered the ancient quote: "shallow waters cannot raise a true dragon", but this did not change Kong Chian's mind. After much discussion, Kong Chian then admitted that another reason why he had turned down the offer was that he still desired to go to the University of Hong Kong to become an engineer. Tan Kah Kee heard this and persisted in offering him the job. Lee Kong Chian promised to seriously consider the offer but wanted to explore other options before making a decision.

## China Floods (1916)

Still undecided about his future on whether to pursue his dream to study engineering, Lee Kong Chian decided to take a break and travel to Medan, Indonesia, to visit his old friends, Zhang Fuying and her husband Lin Jingren (林景仁). When Fuying's father, Zhang Hongnan (张鸿南), heard that Lee Kong Chian wanted to study engineering at the University of Hong Kong, he immediately offered Kong Chian a personal scholarship to pay the university fees. Thanking Zhang Hongnan and now being able to fulfil his ambitions, Lee Kong Chian accepted this kind offer.[3]

While sailing back to Singapore from Indonesia, Lee Kong Chian heard news about floods in China, and he was worried about his father and brothers who were living in the countryside. When Tan Kah Kee met up with Kong Chian soon after his return, he intended to ask Kong Chian if he had made up his mind whether to accept his job offer or study in Hong Kong, but they started talking about the China floods, and Tan Kah Kee told Lee Kong Chian that he was extremely concerned about the floods and had organised a disaster relief campaign among overseas Chinese to donate money to the victims.

On hearing Tan Kah Kee's altruistic act, Lee Kong Chian was deeply moved and decided to give up the scholarship and the opportunity to study at the University of Hong Kong, and to devote himself to Tan Kah Kee's Khiam Aik Company.

## Entering the Rubber Business (1916)

In 1916, Lee Kong Chian started to take charge of Tan Kah Kee's rubber export business. As he was single, he lived in a room next to the shared dormitory where the rubber factory workers lived. His room was cramped, and he had a little table with a canvas camp bed; but there was barely enough space for him to turn around.

During his work, Lee Kong Chian was eager to learn and often asked his factory subordinates for details about the technical problems facing rubber production, the processing techniques, the smoking and fumigation of rubber, etc. He diligently studied the rubber business, and with his innate intelligence, within a relatively short time, he became knowledgeable and familiar with the rubber industry.

Lee Kong Chian was already fluent in both Chinese and English, but in addition, he started to pick up several other languages, so he could make contact and negotiate with other businessmen, both local and foreign. These businessmen soon felt comfortable dealing with Kong Chian, so the company's business advanced by leaps and bounds.

According to Tan Kah Kee's published memoirs, between 1917 and 1920, Khiam Aik Company made an annual profit of about 1 million dollars, which was an astronomical sum in those days. Lee Kong Chian had worked so hard and performed so well that in 1918, despite being in the job for only two short years, Tan Kah Kee promoted him to become the general manager of Khiam Aik Company.

## The Wedding (1920)

Tan Kah Kee liked the talented young Lee Kong Chian, and had started to ask around whether he was married, with the hope that he might be able to match-make him with his eldest daughter, Tan Ai Leh (陈爱礼).

At that time, Lee Kong Chian was not wealthy yet, so questions were raised as to why Tan Kah Kee wanted to choose him as a potential husband for his daughter. One possible reason was the fact that Tan Kah Kee's wife had passed away early, and thus his daughter had no experience living with the older generation, and was therefore not suitable to be married into an established rich family. Hence, Lee Kong Chian, who was single and had no parents in Singapore, was considered an appropriate candidate.

Tan Kah Kee sent someone to visit Lee Kong Chian's countryside home to check that he was unmarried. Upon learning that Lee Kong Chian was still single, he went to consult Xue Wuyuan (薛武院), a mutual friend, and he agreed to be the matchmaker, and introduced Kah Kee's daughter to Kong Chian. The timing was good and Lee Kong Chian himself said that had he been approached earlier, he might have decided to wait a while before accepting the proposal, as he wanted his career to be more established before daring to think of starting a family.

In 1920, Tan Kah Kee's eldest daughter, Tan Ai Leh, was 17 years old and was still studying at Nanyang Girls' School. Lee Kong Chian was then 27 years old and had worked successfully in Tan Kah Kee's rubber export company for four years, and he felt that this was the right time to tie the knot.

Wedding of Lee Kong Chian and Tan Ai Leh (1920); the pair is standing in the centre of the photograph.

The wedding was held at Tao Nan School, where Kong Chian had taught previously. It was officiated and witnessed by Dr. Lim Boon Keng (林文庆, *Lin Wenqing*), a friend of Tan Kah Kee. Dr. Lim Boon Keng was later to become President of Xiamen University (厦门大学). Other witnesses were the honeymoon matchmaker Xue Wuyuan and his relative Xue Zhonghua

(薛中华). The latter would lend his three-story bungalow house in the Katong district to the married couple for their honeymoon.

After the marriage, Tan Kah Kee let his now son-in-law Lee Kong Chian manage all the rubber businesses of Khiam Aik Company. This promotion allowed Kong Chian to gain an even deeper understanding of the rubber business in Malaya. In addition, he was able to observe at close hand the management style and techniques of Tan Kah Kee. In a few short years, Kong Chian was already familiar with all aspects of the export of rubber, its domestic and foreign markets, market conditions, and the financial handling of loans and credits. He also gained a clear understanding of the whole rubber industry, from the planting of rubber trees, the tapping of latex and the production and curing of rubber to make tyres and shoes, to trading operations, price quotation, customs declaration, shipping procedures, etc.

## Banking Business

Lee Kong Chian was highly successful in the rubber business. Thus, on 10 August 1923, Tan Kah Kee sold 100 shares (with a face value of $100 per share) of the Chinese Commercial Bank (华商银行, *Huashang Bank*) he owned to Lee Kong Chian. Tan Kah Kee originally owned a total of 275 shares in this bank, and therefore after selling 100 shares to Lee Kong Chian, he was left with 175 shares for himself. This move demonstrated that Tan Kah Kee was encouraging Lee Kong Chian to expand without affecting the Khiam Aik rubber business, as there were no competing conflicts of interests between banks and the rubber industry.[3]

Four months later, on 12 December 1923, the new shareholder with 100 shares, Lee Kong Chian, was elected as one of the directors of the bank at a shareholders' meeting. This showed that his talent had long been appreciated by the bank. Other directors of the Chinese Commercial Bank were people with close relations to Tan Kah Kee. This included another friend, Lim Nee Soon (林义顺, *Lin Yishun*), the "pineapple king", and Dr. Lim Boon Keng, whom he had appointed as President of Xiamen University. The year 1923 was the peak of Tan Kah Kee's career, with his son-in-law as his right-hand man on the board of a bank, which also enhanced this bank's integrity and trustworthiness.

Lee Kong Chian's appointment onto the board of directors of the Chinese Commercial Bank also improved his status in society and elevated his business reputation. It enabled him to talk directly and at a higher level to other business leaders, and it paved the way for him to start his own business enterprise. It was also the start of his lifelong and inseparable relationship with the banking industry.

Two entrepreneurs, Lim Nee Soon and Yap Geok Twee (叶玉堆, *Ye Yudui*), who later had a significant impact on Lee Kong Chian's career, were both important members of the board of directors of the Chinese Commercial Bank during the same period. Lim Nee Soon was its director and vice chairman and became Lee Kong Chian's mentor, helping him to learn about banking and entrepreneurship. Therefore, Lee Kong Chian's entry into the board of directors of Chinese Commercial Bank was another turning point in his life.

The other member of the board of directors was Yap Geok Twee, who was the son of businessman Ye Dapao (叶大炮), one of the major shareholders and directors of the Chinese Commecial Bank. When Ye Dapao died in 1923, most of his equity was inherited by his son. Yap Geok Twee joined the board of directors in 1926, and he and Lee Kong Chian immediately hit it off. They cooperated closely in the Chinese Commercial Bank and later in the merged Oversea-Chinese Banking Corporation (OCBC).

In 1926, Lee Kong Chian bought another 100 shares of the Chinese Commercial Bank, giving him a total of 200 shares. In 1928, Kong Chian wanted to buy Dayuanqiu (大园丘), a rubber plantation near Muar, so he sold 100 shares of the Chinese Commercial Bank. Then, in 1928, Tan Kah Kee sold his remaining 175 shares to Kong Chian, bringing his total to 275 shares of the bank.

In 1928, Lee Kong Chian succeeded in purchasing Dayuanqiu for $100,000 (which he renamed as Furong Yuan, 芙蓉园), and sold it a couple of years later at a profit of $300,000. With this money, he founded his own company, the Nanyi Rubber Company (南益橡胶公司), which was given the English name Lee Rubber Company in 1931. Kong Chian himself owned $300,000 of this rubber company's shares, while $100,000 of shares were owned by Lim Nee Soon and his son Lin Zhongguo (林忠国).

During the global economic recession in the 1930s, the Nanyi Rubber Company faced financial problems. Fortunately, Yap Geok Twee,

Lee Kong Chian's friend, helped rescue the company by adding shares to the company, which not only overcame the difficulties, but also established a solid reputation for its future development into a world-class rubber business.

The purchase of Dayuanqiu was a turning point for Lee Kong Chian, because without this rubber plantation, he would not have been able to establish his own company, the Nanyi Rubber Company.[4]

This brings us to the story of Lee Kong Chian and the tiger.

## Tiger Mountain

Working in Khiam Aik Company, Lee Kong Chian saved his earnings. But rather than deposit them in a bank to earn interest, he thought it was better to invest his money by buying rubber plantations, an industry where profits were considerable. So, he surveyed the rubber industry and looked around for rubber plantations put up for sale. Kong Chian even released some indication that he was interested in purchasing a rubber plantation so as to test the market.[3]

By good fortune, a British grower living in Muar, Malaya, wanted to return to Britain, and was willing to sell his rubber estate on the cheap. The area was more than 1,000 acres, but he only asked for $100,000, which was less than $100 per acre. In fact, the market value for the location that this rubber estate was in was double the price at $200 per acre. If it had been in a more central location with good transportation, it could have been sold for $300 to $400 per acre.

Once Lee Kong Chian learnt of the British grower's intentions, he immediately visited him at his rubber estate and asked for more details. The British grower saw that Kong Chian was a genuine buyer, and he told him that the price and payment terms could be negotiated on preferential terms. Upon hearing the terms, Lee Kong Chian rushed back to Singapore that very night and told his father-in-law of his intention to buy this rubber plantation.

Tan Kah Kee, being forthright and candid, listened to Lee Kong Chian but straightaway loudly scolded him. He pointed out that this rubber estate was at a mountainous part near Muar where tigers were known to roam, and nobody dared to go up the mountain to tap rubber. The estate had become a wasteland.

Lee Kong Chian sat quietly, listening to his father-in-law admonish him, and then bowing his head, offered him a cup of tea. He waited until Tan Kah Kee's anger had dissipated before expressing his own opinion.

Lee Kong Chian explained that the newspapers reported the government's plans to open new roads nearby to develop the economy of Muar. Once these roads were built and operational, the tigers would likely disappear.

Tan Kah Kee was not convinced by this argument, pointing out the government had been talking about building roads for many years and that it was all talk and no action. He advised Lee Kong Chian not to buy the estate.

Since his father-in-law did not support him, funding the purchase became a problem. However, Lee Kong Chian was confident he could make good profits from the rubber business. His calculation was that 1 kg of rubber latex could be sold at $1, and since 100–200 rubber trees could be grown on 1 acre of land, with each tree producing nearly 8 kg of rubber latex per annum, his 1,000-acre plantation could, therefore, produce roughly 800,000 kg of rubber each year, thus bringing in an income of $800,000. The expenses incurred would include workers' wages, cost of the rubber plants, fertiliser, transport and miscellaneous expenses. Adding this to his initial investment of $100,000 dollars, he calculated that he could recoup his investment in under three years.

Going against the advice of his father-in-law, Lee Kong Chian decided to go ahead, and went to raise the money to buy the rubber estate. First, he sold 100 shares of his Chinese Commercial Bank, then he borrowed money from various sources, but as he could only raise $80,000 dollars, he was still short of $20,000.

Despite this, Lee Kong Chian took the money to the British seller, saying that he could only raise $80,000 at that point in time. However, the Englishman was eager to return to England, and he had long wanted to let go of his rubber plantation; he was also afraid that the matter of "tigers eating people" would be brought to Lee Kong Chian's attention and hence make him change his mind; so he agreed to accept $80,000, and proposed that the remaining $20,000 be paid in instalments. At that time, installment payment was not prevalent, and these terms pleasantly surprised Kong Chian. Finally, the two sides went to the lawyer's office to sign the sales contract, each getting what they wanted, thus completing the transaction.

After the rubber "garden" (Dayuanqiu) was transferred to Lee Kong Chian, he named it "Furong Yuan" in memory of his birthplace in Furong Village, Nan'an County, Fujian Province.

Luckily for Lee Kong Chian, the Malayan government soon built a road near the rubber estate, and the tigers disappeared. The price of the rubber estate soon soared by two to three times, and later, even when someone offered more than $200,000 to buy the land, Kong Chian still did not want to sell.

Finally, someone offered $400,000, which was very attractive, and since Lee Kong Chian could make a profit of $300,000 in such a short period of time, he agreed to sell the rubber plantation, and used the sale proceeds as capital for his Nanyi Rubber Company.

The Chinese in Singapore and Malaya soon began spreading the story that "despite knowing tigers are there, he [Lee Kong Chian] still climbed up Tiger Mountain". Lee Kong Chian must have had such a ferocious spirit and was so blessed by Heaven that even tigers were afraid of him!

## References

1. Yong CF. *Tan Kah-Kee: the Making of an Overseas Chinese Legend*. World Scientific (2014). ISBN: 9789814447898
2. Suryadinata L. *Tan Kah Kee and Lee Kong Chian: in the Making of Modern Singapore and Malaysia*. Chinese Heritage Centre (2010). ISBN 9789810853501
3. Li, Y. R. 李远荣. (1998) *The Memoirs of Lee Kong Chian.* 《李光前传》 香港: 名流出版社. (Call no.: Chinese RSING 959.57 LYR-[HIS])
4. Li, Z., editor (2006). *Lee Kong Chian: A Model of Overseas Chinese*. Guang Da Publisher Ltd Co.

# 3 Rubber

## Nanyi Rubber

With the guidance of Tan Kah Kee, Lee Kong Chian stepped onto the road of business. He not only inherited traditional business techniques but also used his own knowledge, wisdom and talent to open up a new pathway to create a new world in the rubber industry.

Earlier, in 1916, Lee Kong Chian had already given up his ambitions to study at the University of Hong Kong and decided to enter Tan Kah Kee's Khiam Aik Company to learn about the rubber trade. This meant that he voluntarily gave up his desire to become an engineer to start on a different path with different challenges.

Since 1920, Tan Kah Kee had decided to focus on the manufacturing of rubber products while allowing Lee Kong Chian to concentrate on the exporting of these products. Their different investment interests strengthened Kong Chian's entrepreneurial mindset.

The economic situation of Malaya and Singapore and the mobility of Tan Kah Kee's employees in the mid-1920s also triggered Lee Kong Chian to start his own business.

## Price of Rubber

Between 1914 and 1922, the price of natural rubber swung from $0.115 to $1.02 per pound weight. From the 1920s the price of rubber started to drop significantly due in part to overproduction of rubber, and the outlook was worsening. The British government decided to stabilise the price of rubber by limiting the amount of rubber that could be produced and exported, a plan known as the Stevenson Plan.[1] This raised the price of rubber to $1.80 per pound in 1925, and Tan Kah Kee's company profits rose significantly. Some of his old staff, upon seeing that the rubber trade had improved, decided to leave the company to venture out and start their own businesses. Most of these people were originally from the Fujian province and had come to work in Singapore. They formed a tight rubber business network, resulting in the Fujian clan dominating the Singapore rubber industry, thanks in part to Tan Kah Kee. However, countries that depended upon rubber imports were unhappy, and by 1928, the Stevenson Plan was repealed, and there was a return to the free market.

Tan Kah Kee was initially unhappy that his old staff had left his company to start their own rubber export businesses because he thought that they were going to compete against his own company and thereby reduce his profits.

Thus, when he started his own business, Lee Kong Chian was internally conflicted. On one hand, his impulse to start his own business was triggered when he saw his colleagues and subordinates that included Tan Lark Sye (陈六使) start their businesses and do well. On the other hand, he did not want to "put a knife" into his father-in-law; his loyalty prohibited this, especially when he knew about Tan Kah Kee's displeasure over his old employees becoming competitors, which was causing his business to slide. This invisible family responsibility made Kong Chian temporarily restrain his ambition to start a business, delaying his business plan.[2]

Indeed, from 1916 to 1927, Lee Kong Chian worked fulltime for Tan Kah Kee's Khiam Aik Company, and the company's annual profit jumped from $500,000 to $4 million. During this period, he had gained considerable experience managing such a large company, so he started to reconsider starting his own company.

In this context, it is not difficult to understand the caution Lee Kong Chian took and the painstaking effort he made to deal with his entrepreneurial problems. In fact, he was the last to leave Tan Kah Kee towards the latter half of the 1920s. His friend Tan Lark Sye had already left and started the Aik Ho Company (益和公司) in 1924, and it was doing well by 1927.

Eventually, Lee Kong Chian managed to obtain the blessing of Tan Kah Kee to start his own independent company, but it was on condition that he continued to work at Khiam Aik Company, and that it did not interfere with his responsibilities in Kah Kee's company. Therefore, in 1927, Kong Chian and a friend jointly set up and operated a rubber-curing smokehouse in Muar, Johor, Malaya. He bought rubber from small, local rubber plantation owners to make ribbed sheets, which he sold to local or Singapore rubber merchants. This smokehouse processing business did not conflict with Kah Kee's rubber export business but had a complementary benefit. Rubber trade depended on two major factors: the production of rubber and the "consumption" by the foreign markets. For both dealings, the more, the better. Additionally, the ribbed sheets produced by Kong Chian's smokehouse could also be sold to Kah Kee's Khiam Aik Company, thus avoiding a conflict of interest.

The business of the smokehouse was overseen by his business friend in Muar, who served as the manager for 17 years from 1927 until 1944, when tragically he was killed by the Japanese during the Second World War. Lee Kong Chian only took time during weekends to drive to Muar for inspection. On weekdays, he remained at the Khiam Aik Company to handle Tan Kah Kee's rubber trading business. This arrangement was agreed upon, and was the best of both worlds.

The smokehouse at Muar was quite a small business. In 1927 and 1928, the rubber business was maintained at a high level; in 1928, the average price was $0.48 per pound. Although business improved, yet, the turnover was not high, and the profits limited. At this period, Lee Kong Chian apparently still had not used "Nanyi" for the name of his business.

## Lim Nee Soon's Sembawang Rubber Estates

An important factor in the establishment of Nanyi Rubber Company was related to the adversity of Lim Nee Soon's business.[2]

Lim Nee Soon was an early Teochew rubber tree grower. In 1908, he was appointed general manager of the Sembawang Rubber Estates Ltd, which Dr. Lim Boon Keng founded. In 1911, the company operated a rubber "garden" (plantation) and a rubber factory. In 1929, related to the world-wide Great Depression, the rubber economy was also in recession, where the rubber industry collapsed and rubber accumulated in the warehouses unsold, causing heavy losses.

Much of Lim Nee Soon's rubber estate and rubber factory was mortgaged to the Hongkong and Shanghai Banking Corporation (HSBC), and the bank was putting pressure to collect his debts. Lee Kong Chian had often spoken with HSBC directors on behalf of Tan Kah Kee and hence had a good relationship with Xue Zhonghua of HSBC's Investment and Purchasing Department and other senior staff there. Therefore, through the mediation of Kong Chian, Lim Nee Soon's debt to HSBC was successfully resolved, and the rubber estate and the rubber factory were taken over by HSBC. To thank Kong Chian for his help, Lim Nee Soon suggested to HSBC to rent out to Lee Kong Chian his Tongyi Rubber Factory (通益胶厂) located in an area known as Nee Soon Village (renamed Springleaf Park in 2014).

HSBC had no objection as it had always appreciated Lee Kong Chian's talent, and hence agreed to rent it to him on favourable terms. In fact, to find someone to rent a rubber factory at that time was already extremely difficult. Many factories were closing down, and there was a huge surplus of rubber in the rubber industry, causing rubber prices to nosedive.

Lim Nee Soon's only condition when he leased his Tongyi Rubber Factory to Lee Kong Chian was that his son Lin Zhongguo could have a share in Kong Chian's new company, and that they operate the rubber factory together. Since Lin Zhongguo was also Tan Kah Kee's son-in-law (Lin had earlier married one of Tan Kah Kee's daughters) and, therefore, Kong Chian's brother-in-law, both were glad to cooperate with one another; and during an economic downturn, one more partner could certainly reduce individual investment amounts and risk. The new company was named Lee Rubber Company, which was separate from Tan Kah Kee's company. But this created a dilemma for Kong Chian.

## Lee Kong Chian's Dilemma

In 1931, four years after Lee Kong Chian had set up his rubber smokehouse in Muar, he was finally deciding whether or not to completely leave Tan Kah Kee's Khiam Aik Company and devote his entire time to managing his own business. The timing was bad because business was plummeting due to the international economic slowdown. Would those in the social and business community say that he was disloyal to his father-in-law? Furthermore, his previous investments in the Chinese Commercial Bank and his smokehouse were on condition that they would not hinder his responsibilities at Kah Kee's Khiam Aik Company. Now that he was planning to resign his position and start something on his own, would he get his father-in-law's permission and blessing?

Lee Kong Chian's concerns were reasonable, for at the time, Chinese society was still traditional and conservative — Chinese businessmen paid great attention to sincerity, loyalty and moral standards. If things were not settled properly, how could he stand upright and honourable in society and in the business world in future? Hence, before he left, he visited Tan Kah Kee's friends and various seniors in the business community, and one by one, he explained his decision to leave Khiam Aik Company to gain their understanding.

Although Tan Kah Kee did not overtly object to his son-in-law's decision to resign and start his own business, thus becoming a potential competitor, he was quietly unhappy. Fortunately, they did not become enemies, as can be seen by their relationship thereafter. Lee Kong Chian gave Kah Kee strong support when the Hokkien Clan Association was reorganised (1929–1930) and also when Kah Kee's company was reorganised to become a limited company (1931). So apparently, Kong Chian was finally able to gain Kah Kee's understanding.

## Establishing a Business Reputation

When Lee Kong Chian's Nanyi Rubber Company was first set up in 1931, its office was located at 112 Robinson Road located in Singapore's central business district. To process rubber, he rented space from the Tongyi Rubber Factory (originally owned by Lim Nee Soon). Kong Chian was a hard worker, waking up at 4 am every day, putting on his long socks and diagonally striped yellow shorts, and going to supervise the staff at the factory.

At the beginning, Lee Kong Chian's policy was not to buy rubber plantations nor build or buy rubber factories, only renting the rubber factory from Lim Nee Soon, the father of his shareholder Lin Zhongguo. However, he did expand the rubber smokehouse at Muar. Since he did not possess his own rubber orchards, he had to rely on supplies from small rubber estate owners. Facing fierce competition, Lee Kong Chian used cash to buy his rubber and kept to his ethical principle of not cheating anyone. Any member of his staff or workers caught cheating was fired immediately, and the cheated customers would be compensated. This established a trustworthy and principled foundation for the growth of his company.

Lee Kong Chian always made sure that Nanyi Rubber Company had sufficient cash so that not only was the purchasing of rubber paid for with cash, but so too were all items used by the workers in the factory. These items included the workers' food, the latex acid, as well as the wood used for the fire to melt the rubber. He never owed other businesses any money, and in this way, businessmen were willing to give preferential treatment and reduce their selling price to the Nanyi Rubber Company so that the cost of his rubber production would be lower than that of his competitors.

As for the small plantation owners who sold rubber latex and rubber crepes to Nanyi Rubber Company, they received cash on delivery for these items. When they were in urgent need of cash, they could also discuss with the company how much they could borrow on credit. In this way, not only were the urgent needs of small rubber plantation owners addressed, but business was also enhanced. Hence, owners of small rubber estates were glad to trade with Nanyi Rubber Company, and this trust meant that there was minimal risk of interruption or shortage of rubber supplies, which made up for Nanyi Rubber Company not owning any rubber plantations during its early days.

Even Nanyi Rubber Company's branch factories and offices were not allowed to owe one another money in rubber sales and trading. Indeed, all of Lee Kong Chian's companies adopted this policy of cash on delivery, and this minimised mistakes being made. This transparency ensured a clear understanding of the actual financial situation in the branches and offices. So, for many decades, Nanyi Rubber Company had adequate cash and would not welch or default on payment, so their clients and customers were very comfortable doing business with them. It did not owe its customers a penny, and this was a record that the company was proud of in its long history.

Because of this philosophy of total integrity, Nanyi Rubber Company's clients gave it good publicity, and its reputation soared, so much so that more and more customers came to trade with the company. Many small rubber plantation owners who originally dealt with other companies began crossing over and selling their latex and crepe sheets to Nanyi Rubber Company. Therefore, despite fierce competition, Nanyi Rubber Company began knocking down its competitors.

In addition to the acquisition of raw materials, Lee Kong Chian streamlined and improved the sheet production process. This reduced the difficulties his factory workers were facing in moving crepe sheets or latex from one place to another. Not only did it improve their work efficiency, it also reduced the cost of production. Lee Kong Chian also made improvements in smoke room equipment by widening the fire stove, increasing the size of the smoke room, and had all four walls cemented. In this way, the charcoal fire was stronger and hotter, which could make better-quality smoked sheets and produce more layers at the same time.

In the rubber industry, smoked or crepe sheets were graded from 1 to 3, with 1 being the poorest quality (and hence the cheapest) and 3 being the best and the most expensive. Therefore, distinguishing between the quality of the fire-smoked rubber accurately was very important. If the employees of Nanyi Rubber Company were careless or negligent about the classification of the quality of the rubber, the company might either suffer losses or the customers might feel cheated if they were overcharged. Indeed, if a customer complained that the product received did not match the grade assessed, the company would immediately investigate. If verified, the customer would be promptly compensated for the loss. So, Lee Kong Chian would repeatedly tell his employees to be very careful in producing the highest quality of rubber.

Indeed when Lee Kong Chian founded Nanyi Rubber Company, he set down these four cardinal principles in business:

| **Business Principles** | |
|---|---|
| Honesty | 诚实 |
| Trustworthiness | 信用 |
| Discipline | 严明 |
| Prudence | 谨慎 |

His approach to life was also based on these principles; and he employed them in a pragmatic and consistent manner throughout his entire life.

In 1928, a year after the Nanyi Rubber Company was founded, the average price of rubber was 48 cents per pound, but it dropped to 34 cents per pound in 1929, halving its value in 1930 to 15 cents per pound, and in 1932, rubber was sold for only 6 cents per pound. Fluctuations in price were colossal, and if sale pricing was careless, all gains could be eliminated. This was especially so in 1930 when the older generation of rubber magnates went bankrupt one by one.

Because of this, Lee Kong Chian prohibited company staff to engage in short-selling transactions and to only adopt a policy of making less profits but being able to sell more. This allowed Nanyi Rubber Company to make steady gains and progress, enabling it to survive one problem after another and eventually achieve a thriving business.

## Lee Rubber Company Pte Ltd (1931)

In 1929, the world economy was depressed, and latex prices continued to drop. Under pressure from eight banks, led by HSBC, Tan Kah Kee's Khiam Aik Company was restructured on 4 August 1931 to become a limited company. The memorandum for registration was signed by Tan Kah Kee and Lee Kong Chian. Cited as chairpersons of the company's directors were Lee Kong Chian and Yap Geok Twee.

Lee Kong Chian's own company, Nanyi Rubber Company, moved to No. 12 Nangana Road (南干拿路) on 30 June 1931. Given that some companies were facing financial crises and the economy was showing no signs of recovery, Kong Chian also actively prepared to restructure his own company into a limited liabilities company. Two Fujian businessmen, Yap Geok Twee and Li Pishu (李丕树), also added shares to help him develop his business.

Since 1926, Lee Kong Chian and Yap Geok Twee had been managers of the Chinese Commercial Bank, and Kong Chian became the vice-chairman in 1931 when Xue Wuyuan stepped down as vice-chairman. Li Pishu was a native of Nan'an City, Fujian Province, which was where Kong Chian also came from, and Pishu's business in Medan, Sumatra, was flourishing. Yap Geok Twee and Li Pishu admired Kong Chian's talent and loyalty, and were willing to help him overcome the economic downturn of the Great Depression. The formation of a limited company would also limit the debt liabilities of the company. This was the background of the reorganisation of the Nanyi Rubber Company into a limited company at the end of 1931.

On 9 December 1931, Nanyi Rubber Company added a new section with an English name, Lee Rubber Company Pte Ltd, commonly referred to as Lee Rubber. It was jointly registered by Lee Kong Chian and Lin Zhongguo, with a registered capital of $500,000, divided into 5,000 shares at $100 per share. Lee Rubber acquired the business and all the assets of Nanyi Rubber Company. The transfer contract was completed and signed on 28 January 1932 at the purchase price of $639,825.58.

The asset valuation of Nanyi Rubber Company was listed as follows:

| ITEM | AMOUNT |
|---|---|
| Rubber inventory | $563,558.90 |
| Furniture, groceries, etc. | $34,437.88 |
| Bank deposit | $2,465.03 |
| Cash | $3,781.77 |
| Others | $35,582.00 |
| **TOTAL** | $639,825.58 |

Under the contract, the acquisition was carried out in a cash and share exchange procedure. The new Lee Rubber paid $253,025.58 in cash to Nanyi Rubber Company, and the remaining $386,800 was exchanged for 3,868 shares of the new company, worth $100 per share.

Lee Kong Chian had been the major shareholder of the original Nanyi Rubber Company, so he received 3,122 shares of Lee Rubber. The remaining 746 shares were allocated as follows: his wife, Tan Ai Leh, received 250 shares; his partner, Lin Zhongguo, received 339 shares; his brother, Li Yurong, received 100 shares, and the remaining 57 shares were distributed between three senior employees. From its capital structure after the reorganisation, Lee Rubber was basically still a family business — Kong Chian was the largest shareholder, with his family (his own shares plus his wife and brother) owning 3,472 shares, or 89% of the registered capital.

In the early stage of the reorganisation, although Yap Geok Twee and Li Pishu did not have any shares, Geok Twee and Pishu's son Li Chengchong (李成崇) were appointed as two of the three directors (the remaining director was Lee Kong Chian).

In June 1933, Lee Rubber increased its registered capital to $1 million, and the paid-up capital was $560,000. Lee Kong Chian's shares also increased to 3,723 shares, with Lin Zhongguo now owning 340 shares; Kong Chian's wife and brother's shares were unchanged. Lee Kong Chian's family remained the majority shareholder with 4,073 shares, or 72% of paid-in capital. Li Pishu's family was the second largest shareholder with 840 shares, or 15% of the paid-up capital. Yap Geok Twee only made a symbolic investment.

After Lee Rubber got Yap Geok Twee and Li Pishu to add shares, its foundation became solid, and the company began to enter its developmental stage. After the reorganisation, economic trends, domestic and foreign, were also conducive to the development of Lee Rubber in the rubber industry.

In 1928, the price of rubber was 48 cents per pound. But the world economic recession badly affected the rubber business, so that by 1932, this Great Depression had entered its lowest ebb. Rubber prices bottomed out at 6 cents per pound. Big and small rubber estates, one by one, stopped tapping, ceased production, and laid off staff. Many rubber manufacturers and rubber factories also closed. By the end of the year, Singapore was left with only a few large-scale rubber businesses. Within a couple more years, big entrepreneurs found that they had over-borrowed and could not repay their debts, and in 1934, Tan Kah Kee decided to close Khiam Aik Company. The closure of rubber businesses meant that competition was reduced, and under the operating principle of small profits and quick turnover, Lee Kong Chian began to set up his rubber collection and sales networks. In the following year, prices started recovering.

In mid-1933, the governments of Britain, France, Holland and Thailand had decided to implement an international agreement to restrict the production of rubber to keep the price of rubber stable between 20 cents and 38 cents per pound and this price control continued from 1934 to 1941. From 1934, with the world economy beginning to recover from worldwide recession and with rubber prices being stabilised, demand for rubber gradually increased in industrial countries like Europe and America.

## Expansion of Lee Rubber

After reorganising Khiam Aik Company into a limited liabilities company in 1931, Tan Kah Kee had begun to gradually shrink his business, which included closing, renting or selling the less profitable and underperforming sectors. These measures benefited Lee Rubber greatly. Lee Kong Chian's conservative approach of not overreaching his resources or stockpiling rubber meant that he had significant financial reserves and did not owe any money. By 1932 he was one of the three rubber companies that survived the Great Depression. He then took advantage of the plunging prices affecting his failing rival companies by buying them up at rock bottom prices. It was during this period (1931–1934) that Lee Rubber acquired Fudong Rubber Company (福东树胶公司) in Indonesia from Tan Kah Kee and also rented his rubber factories in Singapore, Penang and Klang. In 1934, Lee Rubber ventured further and set up a branch warehouse in Thailand, the Siam Pakthai Company. To manage rubber exports to the United States, he set up the South Asia Corporation in New York.

On the eve of the outbreak of the Pacific War in 1941, Lee Rubber had four rubber factories in the following areas of Singapore: Seletar, Tanjong Rhu, Kallang Road and Bukit Timah. It also had branch warehouses and rubber factories in major commercial ports on the coast of Malaya, such as in Muar, Penang, Klang and Malacca and branches in Seremban, Kuala Lumpur and Teluk Intan. Lee Rubber also owned two large rubber companies in Medan and Palembang, Sumatra, which were the main rubber-producing areas in Indonesia. Under the Fudong Rubber Company headquartered in Palembang, South Sumatra, there were also branch warehouses and rubber factories in Jambi, Pontianak and Banjarmasin. It also owned another company, Fuli (福利公司), which was located in Medan, an important town in North Sumatra, which had rubber factories in Langsa, Sibolga, Ashahan and Lando. In Thailand, a company responsible for collecting rubber produced in the country was set up.

In terms of market sales, Lee Rubber had very early on directly exported rubber to Europe and the United States and had agents in the two major world rubber market centres in New York and London. On 15 January 1934, Lee Rubber's head office moved to the China Building (Hua Xia, 华厦, now the OCBC Building) along Chulia Street, Singapore (see figure on page 52).

Lee Kong Chian also invested in the pineapple and biscuit industry before the Second World War. He established Lee Pineapple Co Ltd on 9 December 1931 to acquire the business and capital of Nanyi Pineapple Company.

The Hongkong and Shanghai Banking Corporation (HSBC) strongly supported Lee Kong Chian, and was a big factor in Lee Rubber's rapid growth from 1931 to 1941. As mentioned above, Kong Chian's good relationship with HSBC stemmed from the fact that he had worked with Tan Kah Kee, who had also been supported by HSBC. Later, when Kah Kee's company was reorganised, on behalf of the Chinese Commercial Bank and together with HSBC's representative, Kong Chian served as a director in Kah Kee's reorganised company. His clear distinction between public and private dealings won the appreciation and trust of senior managers of HSBC, and obtained for him overdraft allowances and financial loans when, in 1934 and 1936, Lee Rubber overdrew $215,000 and $155,000 from HSBC, respectively, for investment purposes. Hence, Lee Kong Chian's former principles of no borrowing or lending were now being relaxed.

## Tan Kah Kee's Khiam Aik Company

Seriously hit by the economic downturn during the Great Depression of the early 1930s, Tan Kah Kee's Khiam Aik Company suffered heavy losses, and it was finally taken over by eight banks led by the Hongkong and Shanghai Banking Corporation (HSBC) on 4 August 1931 and closed in 1934.

Lim Nee Soon's Tongyi Rubber Factory also owed a lot of money to HSBC, and was already facing difficulties. In 1928, his rubber business and factory was taken over by HSBC.

Why did Tan Kah Kee's rubber business fail? There were two major reasons.

First, there was no bonus system for his employees to keep them happy. Every time the company made substantial profits, employees had to haggle for more pay. Although they were earning quite a lot, they were still not satisfied, so a large number of employees left his company to set up their own businesses and competed with him, which was to prove detrimental for his company.

Second, the global economy went into recession in the late 1920s to the 1930s. When Tan Kah Kee was managing his rubber business from 1916 up to 1925, it was still profitable, earning, on average, $1 million a year. From 1925 to 1932, the cost of rubber fell from a high of $1.80 per pound to 6 cents per pound. In Singapore, 45 out of the 46 rubber factories had to close, leaving only one survivor. Thus, the global economic downturn contributed to Tan Kah Kee's failure.

From left to right: Tan Kah Kee, Lee Kong Chian, and Tan Lark Sye (photo taken around the 1950s).

How did Lee Kong Chian survive? His Nanyi Rubber Company was also hit hard by the Great Depression, and he lost a lot of his sales. Fortunately, the company's policy of not borrowing or lending money meant that it did not owe huge amounts of money to the banks. Also, Nanyi Rubber Company did not own any rubber plantations or large factories, so its losses were not as heavy as other companies. Plus, during this bleak period, it had the support of Yap Geok Twee and Li Pishu, so the company had sufficient funds to survive.

When Tan Kah Kee's rubber factories in Singapore, Penang and Klang suffered losses and were taken over by HSBC, Lee Kong Chian decided to support these factories by renting them from the bank. When the world economy started to recover, Lee Rubber bought over Tan Kah Kee's Fudong Rubber Company in Palembang, Indonesia, which the bank had also taken over. Around the same time, Lee Rubber also expanded its business to Thailand in 1934. In that year alone, Lee Rubber made a profit of $4 million, and it immediately acquired the rubber plantations and rubber factories of Tan Kah Kee and Lim Nee Soon, which were earlier taken over by HSBC. In this way, Lee Rubber dominated the rubber market, and Lee Kong Chian became the new "Rubber King".

Lee Kong Chian had insight and belief that the world economy would recover in due course, and that rubber prices would rise concomitantly. During the recession, rubber prices were at its lowest of 6 cents per pound, but as the world economy recovered in the mid-to-late 1930s, the price of rubber rose to 20 cents per pound. So he expanded his capital and obtained a bank loan as working capital, hoarding the lower-priced rubber so that when the price of rubber rose, he would make good profits.

Lee Kong Chian explained that his success depended half upon hard work and the other half on opportunities. His diligence was undeniable, but the opportunities he had created was through the integration of his profound knowledge and extraordinary vision.

By the late 1930s, before the start of the Second World War, Lee Kong Chian had already become a business success and a social leader in Singapore and Malaya.

## The Fudong Rubber Company, Palembang, Indonesia

The Fudong Rubber Company in Palembang, Indonesia, was founded in 1900 by the Dutch at a cost of $8 million, with a large rubber plantation and rubber factory. But due to poor management, it had been jointly contracted over to two Chinese, both having the same surname, "Ou", but originating from different provinces of China; one was from Fujian (福建), and the other from Canton (广东, *Guangdong*), so they decided to adopt one character from the names of each of these two China provinces and thus named their company "Fudong" (福东). Later, because of heavy debts, they sold their company to Tan Kah Kee.

In 1931, the Fudong Rubber Company was again facing financial difficulties, and when Tan Kah Kee's business went bankrupt in 1934, the Fudong Rubber Company, together with other branches of his business, was bought over by Lee Kong Chian's newly merged bank, the Oversea-Chinese Banking Corporation (OCBC) for just $20,000. After restoration, Fudong Rubber Company started to become highly profitable.

In the years leading up to the 1930s, Lee Kong Chian had been building up his reputation and was regarded as an important figure in the rubber industry, as well as a name in the cultural, educational and financial circles. Lee Rubber also benefited from its boss being a "hot" Chinese leader, as it was easier for the group to obtain financing from banks. As a result, the Lee Rubber's business expanded rapidly.

It was at this point in time that Lee Kong Chian also started to invest in pineapple plantations and developed the canning industry for the pineapples grown. Eventually, Lee Kong Chian acquired the names "Rubber King" and "Pineapple King".

## Appointments

Lee Kong Chian was appointed to head several organisations, both commercial as well as non-commercial. In 1934, he became the chairman of the Chinese High School, and he also became the chairman of the Hua Chiao (Huaqiao) Middle School that same year.

In 1936, Kong Chian became the chairman of the Fengshan Temple Trust Committee of the Nan'an people.

In 1937, he and Tan Lark Sye actively organised the Rubber Guild to seek better welfare for colleagues in the industry. In 1939, he was elected president of the Singapore Chinese Chamber of Commerce.

All these appointments gave him the opportunity to demonstrate his outstanding leadership abilities.[5,6]

## References

1. Wikipedia. *The Stevenson Plan*. https://en.wikipedia.org/wiki/Stevenson_Plan
2. Li, Y. R. 李远荣. (1998) *The Memoirs of Lee Kong Chian*.《李光前传》 香港: 名流出版社. (Call no.: Chinese RSING 959.57 LYR-[HIS])
3. Nor-Afidah Abd Rahman and Wee, J. Lee Kong Chian, *Singapore Infopedia*. https://eresources.nlb.gov.sg/infopedia/articles/SIP_978_2006-06-16.html
4. Wikipedia. *Lee Kong Chian*. https://en.wikipedia.org/wiki/Lee_Kong_Chian
5. Chew, M. (1996). *Leaders of Singapore*. Singapore: Resource Press, p. 24. (Call no.: RSING 920.05957 CHE)
6. National University of Singapore. *Our chancellors: Speeches and biographical sketch (Lee Kong Chian)*. http://www.lib.nus.edu.sg/nusbiodata/bioleekc.htm (Retrieved: 12 May 2016)

# 4 Labour Relations

## Introduction

The most important appraisal of Lee Kong Chian comes down to his character. He had the highest integrity with absolute honesty and was kind and generous to his colleagues and to those in need. He was intelligent, a good judge of character, and a good leader.

Lee Kong Chian's character can be ascertained by observing how he behaved and interacted with people. Let us first look at how he dealt with his colleagues and workers and how he attained excellent labour relationships, which proved to become the foundation of his business enterprise and development. We shall focus on his Lee Rubber company.

## Staff Recruitment

To join Lee Rubber, one might usually be introduced by an active staff member or recommended by the principal of a Chinese secondary or high school, the latter being students whose academic results were in the top ten and who were also hardworking and held high integrity. After an assessment and interview, successful candidates would be sent to the rubber factories and offices for two-year internships, only after which they would be selected for full-time employment.[1]

During the internship, these young students would learn all the business related to rubber, including the production process, the assessment of rubber quality, rubber technology, refining latex, smoking rubber, and how to distinguish the grades of rubber sheets. Therefore, each staff in Lee Rubber, from the clerk to the manager, had to become like the folklore monk in the Shaolin Temple, who could only emerge after avoiding being whacked by wooden mechanical warriors lining the narrow alley leading to the outside. In other words, the students and staff had to fully understand all the theories and practices of the entire rubber industry before becoming qualified.

Promotions and transfers of employees depended on their assessments and performances at work. After the war, their treatment was already regarded as being better than other companies, and Lee Rubber was considered to be the "golden rice bowl" job.

By 1947, after Lee Rubber had recovered from the Second World War, the management staff there earned between $1,000 and $2,000 a month, which was considered enviable in those days. Later, because of rising prices and inflation, salaries were adjusted; for example, the starting salary of a management staff became $3,000 per month. Each manager was also supplied with a car, while petrol and medical expenses were handled by the company. During this period, the highest monthly salary at Lee Rubber was more than $6,000 for senior staff who had rendered outstanding service.

The most exhilarating time of each year for Lee Rubber employees was during New Year, because every employee would receive a red envelope. Each branch, rubber factory, and warehouse was financially independent in accounting and self-responsible for its profits and losses. But even for a less profitable branch or factory, each employee would still receive a bonus equivalent to two months' salary.

Lee Rubber did not adopt a policy of firing employees. Instead, they were asked to resign if they were found to have committed fraud or made a grave error. However, if a branch lost money for three consecutive years, the branch manager would be considered incompetent, and he would have only one way to go; that is, he would be asked to find another job. Also, for those who were managing factories or were heads of warehouses, if three consecutive months of continuous deficits appeared, they would also be transferred, and new replacements would take over to find out the crux of the loss and remedy the situation.

## Hiring School Students

Why did Lee Kong Chian prefer to hire middle and high school students rather than college or university graduates? The answer was that he believed the former could work more comfortably and be better trained as apprentices in the rubber industry, whereas college graduates would be overqualified. Weighing rubber bales, inspecting latex, smoking rubber sheets and grading them were tasks that school students could perform quite well. Also, there were fewer college and university students during those days, and highly educated graduates tended to flatter themselves as being scholar-officials — many tended to be arrogant and disdained handling dirty and smelly rubber. Furthermore, it would also not be easy for university graduates to work closely or socialise with uneducated rubber plantation and factory workers, and an estrangement barrier might form between them.

In its early days, Lee Rubber tried out some college graduates, but these employees left halfway and their performance was poor. Thereafter, Lee Rubber focused on hiring Chinese secondary and high school students and did not consider taking in university graduates.

There was also a time that when professionals were employed to work as department managers, the results were mediocre. Lee Rubber once hired a retired judge to lead the planning on housing development; they were hoping to take advantage of the judge's experience and social position to achieve housing development objectives. However, the judge was overly strict and pedantic, and so the officials who worked with him went strictly by the law, and everything had to be done by the book. The result was that draft proposals and maps presented for approval kept being delayed over minor wording issues. The retired judge eventually voluntarily resigned because of his slow and over-meticulous bureaucratic approach. Later, the company switched to employing a secondary school graduate who knew the tricks of the trade and could get things done more quickly. This was also one of the reasons for the lack of college graduates and professionals among Lee Rubber employees.

However, with rapid advances in science and technology, the number of professionals employed by Lee Rubber increased, partly because there was need for management to become more professional and also because some departments needed specialised talents and expertise.

## Courteous to Subordinates, Recognising Their Talents

It was not unusual for subordinates who complain excessively to elicit the ire of their bosses, and they might even get fired.

Here was how Lee Kong Chian dealt with an argumentative young lawyer named Chen Sen-Mao (陈森茂). Kong Chian's focus was on hiring talented individuals, so he offered Chen Sen-Mao a job as a manager drawing the highest salary for Lee Rubber. All business contracts and important documents for the company were to be written by Chen and then submitted to Kong Chian for approval and implementation.

Lee Kong Chian's working style had always been one of extreme caution, and he often added or deleted sentences on the file documents that Chen Sen-Mao sent in. Little did he know that this document type had a certain format, and it was quite inconvenient for anyone to change the wording or format. On one occasion, a document sent to Kong Chian was changed again, and Chen Sen-Mao was very upset by this, so he hurried to confront Kong Chian, thrusting the document in front of him, suggesting that if he understood the law, he should draft the document himself. Instead of losing his temper, Kong Chian explained that he was only making suggestions and that Chen Sen-Mao should continue writing the documents.

From then on, Lee Kong Chian gave Chen Sen-Mao full power to handle the relevant legal documents without interference, so the two sides cooperated happily.

This anecdote noting Lee Kong Chian's honest and frank treatment of his colleagues without being overbearing has been cited as the hallmark of a great boss being tolerant and appreciative of talent.

## Management Style

Lee Rubber's management style was unique, being an amalgamation of both Chinese and Western approaches. In the 1950s to the 1960s, of its roughly 3,000 employees, most were middle school students, and very few were college graduates or professionals — they would rather train their employees themselves.

Over the decades, Lee Rubber had developed into a multinational company with a capital of over one billion dollars, with a business encompassing rubber, palm oil, pineapple, banking, real estate, housing construction, and stock investment. They owned about 30 rubber and palm oil business units. In addition to its branches in Singapore, Malaysia, Indonesia and Thailand, the group also had branches in Hong Kong, the United Kingdom and the United States.[2,3]

By 2000, its annual profits exceeded $100 million, which attracted outsiders to study Lee Rubber's management style, and how it managed to fuse eastern and western management and operational modes.

The traditional Chinese system of finding staff was to have an introducer who was familiar with the candidate and understood his personality, character, and family background. Lee Rubber would take into account the accuracy of the introducer's reference and assess the candidate through an interview. Because the rubber industry was one that was prone to frequent cheating and fraud, Lee Kong Chian placed considerable weight on the honesty and credibility of the candidate. It was the hope that by getting an employee through the recommendation of a known introducer, recruiting the wrong candidate might be less likely.

Despite being very busy taking care of many things daily, Lee Kong Chian attached great importance to the quality of the staff he was hiring. If someone sent in an application, he would personally interview the candidate. Kong Chian was highly observant, and during the conversation with the applicant, he could gain insight into the person's integrity, abilities and intelligence. He would record his opinions, and often his judgement would be proven correct in due course.

Whenever a Lee Rubber staff mentioned their experience of being "looked at" by Lee Kong Chian, they often expressed their admiration of his powers of observation and the astute questions he would ask. According to a male employee, Lee Kong Chian asked him during his interview if he liked climbing trees and if he had ever stolen fruits from other people's fruit trees. The candidate said "no", but Kong Chian pointed to the scars on his hands, evidence that he must have had climbed trees as a child; and as for stealing other people's fruits, Kong

Chian said that he knew of no child who did not steal fruits from another person's trees. Kong Chian then warned the young man that he had to be honest and not cheat others if he were to be employed by Lee Rubber. The newcomer was later hired, and he absolutely admired Kong Chian's character and philosophy.

After Lee Kong Chian retired, his eldest son, Lee Seng Gee, served as Chairman of the Lee Rubber. He also followed his father's tradition of interviewing new staff in person.

## Life Employment

In the world of rubber in Singapore and Malaysia, there was a saying: "No-one has the ability to take away the staff of Lee Rubber".

Employees working in Lee Rubber would not leave the company halfway. After they entered into its service, they often remained until they passed on years later. The company adopted a lifetime employment philosophy, and many of their staff who had worked for decades continued to serve in Lee Rubber, even those well past the retirement age of 55 years, which was Singapore's mid-20$^{th}$ century practice.

A good example was Li Chengfeng (李成枫), who joined Lee Rubber in 1929; even when he was over 80 years old, he still held an important position in the company before he passed on. Another example was Tan Sri Dr. Li Wenchen (李文琛), who followed Li Chengfeng as the head of the Malayan Lee Rubber, and he had a long history of working more than 40 years in this company.

Lee Kong Chian had always respected the philosophical and ethical philosophy of Confucius, and in his later years, he also embraced Taoist ideals. The central tenets of Confucianism are the four cardinal principles and eight virtues, which include love, respecting the wise and virtuous, care for the elderly, and prudence. Therefore, Lee Rubber's personnel management and employment policies could not be separated from these principles. Deriving from the Confucian concept of benevolence, Lee Rubber did its best to take care of the welfare of its employees, and its lifelong employment system was closely related to respecting the virtuous and respecting the wiser and older generation.

## Home Ownership

Under Lee Rubber's personnel management and hiring policy, the most noteworthy aspect was its "home ownership" plan. Under this scheme, every employee of the Lee Rubber family would get to be the owner of their own property. Lee Rubber would first lend individual employees a total amount of three years' salary to buy a home, though the owner of the deed would still be Lee Rubber. Then, during the company's annual year-end bonus exercise, the employee's year-end bonus would be deducted by half, of which one half would serve as repayment of the company's housing loan, and this continued until the loan was paid off. Once this happened, the ownership was transferred to the employee. Under this plan, the employee's monthly salary was not affected, so it would not alter the employee's take-home pay and lifestyle.

When an employee resigned, this loan (or whatever remained of it) had to be paid off in one lump sum before the company would change the name on the title deed to the employee's. Therefore, if this employee wanted to seek another job, they had to find a huge amount of money to repay the company before they could become the legal owner of the home.

However, since Lee Rubber treated its staff well, and its bonuses were generous, and the home ownership plan very attractive, Lee Rubber staff would say in Hokkien: "We would not leave our job unless we were beaten to death."

This housing loan scheme preceded the 1968 Singapore government's Housing and Development Board's loan scheme where part of the Central Provident Fund taken from one's salary was used to repay the housing loan.

## Retirement Pension

Among large Chinese organisations, Lee Rubber was hitherto the only one that provided retired employees with pension benefits. The company's philosophy was one of lifetime employment, where their employees could continue to work even after the retirement age of 55. However, for the really elderly workers, the company would require them to retire and stay safe to enjoy their retirement. Upon retirement, employees could still receive a monthly salary equivalent to half their monthly pay at the time of leaving.

According to Lai Zhu San (赖祝三), who worked as a manager at the Lee Rubber Factory in Bukit Pasir, Muar, where Lee Rubber originated, as he had worked for this company all his life, he could enjoy receiving a retirement pension that was not available in other private companies.

Lai came from China in 1935, and began working in Lee Rubber when he was 20 and worked for 47 years before retiring in 1982. He was originally transferred from Penang to the rubber factory at Muar, established in 1937, and he served as its manager for 17 years. He commented that as long as one worked hard and did his job properly, he would not be treated badly.

In order to take care of the welfare of employees and their lives after retirement, Lee Rubber implemented an employee provident fund system in 1951 — this scheme started three years earlier than the Singapore government's Central Provident Fund (CPF).

This system was named "The Maintenance Fund", but its original purpose and structure was very similar to the CPF. Under the Maintenance Fund, employees had 5% of their monthly salary deducted each month, while Lee Rubber forked out an additional 10%, which was added to the fund. This maintenance fee was then deposited monthly into a special bank account kept by the general manager of each administrative region.

Later, when Singapore and then Malaysia implemented the employee provident fund system, the maintenance money that was initially kept by the company was then transferred under the names of the company's staff.

## Bonus Schemes

When Lee Rubber became a limited company in 1931, it adopted the Western management style by rewarding its employees through granting them company shares. As a result, some senior staff members at the Singapore head offices, such as Chen Jimin (陈济民) and Yang Jindian (杨金殿), owned 25 and 10 shares in Lee Rubber, respectively. Later, Lee Rubber changed its system, and instead of giving shares, it gave its workers and staff generous bonuses and incentives.[1]

In order to give their employees a sense of belonging and to improve work efficiency, Lee Rubber allocated 20% of the huge profits it made in 1950 as the year-end bonus for employees. Ordinary branch managers and rubber factory managers that year received bonuses ranging from $300,000 to $500,000, while senior staff received up to $3 million. Because housing and land prices were relatively low in the 1950s, these employees bought land and properties after receiving their huge bonuses. So when the price of land and property rose, many Lee Rubber employees became millionaires; there were even a few billionaires among them.

Some Lee Rubber employees eventually thought of starting their own businesses, and Lee Kong Chian did not stop them. He believed that as long as these businesses did not conflict with Lee Rubber, he agreed to give these employees the freedom to start their own businesses; and perhaps these new businesses might even complement Lee Rubber.

Therefore, Li Chengfeng, the head of Lee Rubber looking after middle and north Malaya, not only founded Nanfeng Engineering Co Ltd (南风工程有限公司) but also founded Liancheng (连成) and Lianxing (联兴) Rubber Companies (树胶有限公司). Lianxing Rubber Company was established in 1955, and it opened four rubber factories in Pontian, Tampin and Kuala Lumpur.

Yang Fengnian (杨逢年) and Huang Guangming (黄光明), the heads of the Fudong Company of the Indonesian administrative region, established the Anshun Company (安顺公司) in Singapore in 1957 to acquire and ship rubber from Jambi, Kalimantan and Banjarmasin to Singapore for sale.

Another senior employee of Lee Rubber Singapore, Tang Kiong Chun (陈共存), a managing director and cousin of Lee Kong Chian, founded South Asia Local Products Limited after the Second World War.

When these senior personnel went out from Lee Rubber to engage in the rubber business, Lee Kong Chian did not express displeasure or ask them to refrain from competition. On the contrary, having gone through the Second World War and difficult times together, and although they were nominally employer and employees, they regarded and treated each other more like brothers. They were good friends, and Kong Chian would discuss matters with them in advance before making final decisions. Lee Kong Chian's three sons, Seng Gee, Seng Tee, and Seng Wee, also treated their father's old heroes with much deference and respect, often consulting them for their views and opinions.

These senior employees, when engaged in rubber activities, were thought to be competing with Lee Rubber; but in reality, they assisted Lee Rubber's businesses, as their companies' activities and business scope were in territories not covered by Lee Rubber.

The Lianxing Rubber Company, founded by Li Chengfeng, later became a subsidiary of Lee Rubber, which owned a 95% stake in the company.

The Anshun Company, founded by Yang Fengnian and Huang Guangming, also became a member of Lee Rubber in 1968. After becoming a subsidiary of Lee Rubber, Yang Fengnian and Huang Guangming remained as shareholders.

South Asia Local Products Limited was originally shared by Tang Kiong Chun and Lee Rubber. Later, when Tang Kiong Chun founded Yanfang Company, Lee Rubber withdrew from South Asia Local Products, and Yanfang Company became a subsidiary of Lee Rubber in 1970, engaging in latex processing also with Standard Malaysian Rubber (SMR).

This was how Lee Rubber let its employees start their own businesses without them directly competing with or hindering its business. On one hand, these employees were allowed to fulfil their aspirations and to display their talents, and on the other hand, it made up for areas that Lee Rubber could not take care of. Eventually, the companies founded by these employees were all integrated into Lee Rubber and became members of Lee Rubber.

The net result of the home ownership, retirement pension, and the generous bonus schemes, coupled with a mindset of lifelong employment, helped deter most employees from leaving Lee Rubber. They were proud to work for this company.

## Entry Refusal

Lee Kong Chian often went to his rubber factories to inspect them. On one occasion, he went to Palembang, Indonesia, on a Sunday to inspect his rubber factory, but he had not informed the manager he was coming. When he arrived at the factory, the main iron gate was locked, and there was an Indian guard on duty. He asked the doorman to let him in but was refused entry. Kong Chian explained that he was the boss from Singapore, but the guard did not believe him because Kong Chian was wearing plain clothes and driving an old Ford car. The guard explained the rules were that unidentified strangers could not be allowed into the factory. Then he asked Kong Chian to leave, otherwise he would call the police. At that moment, one of the workers came out and instantly recognised Kong Chian and told the guard that he was indeed their boss. Frightened, the guard knelt in front of Kong Chian asking for forgiveness, fearing that he would lose his job. But instead of firing him, Kong Chian praised him for being faithful to his duties and for obeying the manager's instructions, and he took out a ten-dollar note from his bag to reward him.

Lee Rubber Building, Kuala Lumpur, constructed in 1930.

Lee Kong Chian endorsed people who were honest and followed rules. He treated all his officers and branch managers with sincerity. From 1947, the administrative and financial authority of the local branches were independent. On the premise of not violating decisions from the head office, the heads of each branch were free to exert their autonomy. The branches in Malaya were under the jurisdiction of Lee Rubber (Selangor)

Co Ltd, with Li Chengfeng being in charge before 1957. Yang Fengnian was in charge of seven rubber factories across Indonesia. All the business in Thailand was managed by Li Yintong.

There were about 30 branches and rubber factories in Malaya, Indonesia and Thailand, bringing in a profit of 40 to 50 million dollars each year.

Outsiders evaluating the success of Lee Rubber believed that in addition to Lee's unique vision and foresight and his ability to create and seize opportunities, his appointment of people on merit and knowing how best to deploy them, was also one of the factors of Lee Rubber's success.

After Lee Kong Chian retired in September 1954 and until he passed away on 2 June 1967, he entrusted the execution and management rights of Lee Rubber to his eldest son Lee Seng Gee, with Kong Chian staying on to act as a consultant. The business of Lee Rubber continued to expand.

## Frugal Lifestyle

Even when Lee Kong Chian became a billionaire, he still maintained a very frugal life. He remembered both the bitter and the sweet parts of his childhood, and he educated his children by citing his own experiences of his hard life in Furong Village, Fujian, China. When he left school and returned to Singapore in 1912 at the age of 19, his father had already returned to his hometown in China. So Kong Chian lived alone in Singapore without any relatives or friends. He had tasted the bitterness of the world, and this helped him understand other people, but it also affected his own behaviour and lifestyle.[4,5]

Lee Kong Chian's life was simple and disciplined. He never drank alcohol or smoked cigarettes. He preferred to travel by bus, take very short lunch breaks and eat simple and cheap meals.

A school friend Tan Ee Leong (陈维龙, *Chen Weilong*) recalled an occasion when he was travelling by a tram, which had seats arranged from first class to third class. As a student, Ee Leong travelled by the cheaper second class seats, but he spotted Lee Kong Chian, who was already the manager of Tan Kah Kee's Company, sitting in a third class seat. "I felt so embarrassed, because he was already working, (and) I was still a student," Ee Leong recalled.

When Lee Kong Chian drove, he would drive an old car. He also did not have a chauffeur. He was a regular blood donor, and on his 70th birthday, he even went out to donate blood before returning to a party organised to celebrate his birthday.

Lee Kong Chian's life of frugality adds further stature to this great individual.

## Bringing Up Children

In 1920, Lee Kong Chian married Tan Ai Leh, the eldest daughter of Tan Kah Kee. Tan Ai Leh was only 17 years old and 10 years younger than him. She was a top student at Nanyang Girls Secondary School and was virtuous and courteous and worthy of her name "爱礼" (meaning "love propriety"), and she was praised by her friends and seniors. Although Kong Chian had thrown himself into the business world, he led a simple life and was most afraid of meaningless entertainment. He went to bed early and got up early, living decades likewise to each single day, and no mahjong tiles ever surfaced in his two-generational home.

Lee Kong Chian (standing, centre) and his wife Tan Ai Leh (seated) with their six children.

Lee Kong Chian and Tan Ai Leh had six children — three boys and three girls — and they were initially given a Chinese education and then prepared for overseas studies. Their eldest daughter, Lee Seok Keng (李淑卿), was sent to high school in Melbourne, Australia, and stayed there during the Second World War. She then studied medicine in Singapore and subsequently worked in London, England, where she met her future husband, Jack William Hoe, also a doctor,

The second daughter, Seok Tin (淑珍), went to high school in the United States and later to Wellesley College during the Second World War. After the war, she left Wellesley College and enrolled in the University of Malaya, which was based in Singapore during that time. She graduated in liberal arts and education and served in the world of education for many years. Upon retirement, she was active in charity and community service.

The third daughter, Seok Chee (淑志), studied fine arts at Smith College in the United States and obtained a Master in Art Education at Columbia University. On returning to Singapore, she taught art history at the Singapore Polytechnic and later became a curator at the National Museum of Singapore.

The eldest son, Seng Gee (成义), studied Business Administration at the University of Pennsylvania's Wharton School. Seng Gee, Seng Wee (成伟, Kong Chian's youngest son), Seok Tin and Seok Chee were in the United States during the Second World War, but because of travel restrictions, were unable to return to Singapore until after the war. Seng Wee and Seok Chee had not entered university yet at that time. Lee Kong Chian and his wife had also been in New York just before the war started to attend a rubber conference.

The second son, Seng Tee (成智), was in Singapore when the war started. He wanted to join his parents and study in the United States, but while on his way there, his boat was bombed and sunk by the Japanese. Luckily he survived and hid in an island off Sumatra. A loyal Lee Rubber employee helped him return to Singapore, where he lived during the war with Lee Kong Chian's brother. When the war ended, he went to study Finance and Business at the University of Pennsylvania's Wharton School, after which he went for further studies at Washington University's McDonnell International Scholars Academy.

Lee Seng Wee studied engineering at the University of Toronto, Canada, and he also obtained an MBA from the University of Western Ontario. Upon graduation he became a manager in the rubber business. After a few years, he was appointed to sit on OCBC's board of management, and eventually he became Chairman. The three brothers worked in Lee Rubber, and each brother looked after separate businesses such as rubber, banking, property and pineapple as well as the Lee Foundation.

Lee Kong Chian did not pursue the extended family system; when his children got married, they moved out of the ancestral house, and their families lived separately. This western small family system did not weaken the children's filial piety toward their parents. Indeed the Lee family's strong filial piety gave the family a sense of mission to protect, maintain and expand their family's assets, business and reputation. This family philosophy produced a code of conduct among the children based on the interests of the family, thus forming a cohesion centred on the assets of the family.

In their private lives, the children followed their own calling, and each had their own interests; for example, they would swim at the seaside bungalow, read books and newspapers and plant flowers, or they would collect calligraphies, paintings and antiques.

Lee Kong Chian at his eldest daughter Lee Seok Keng's wedding in 1953.

## References

1. Li, Y. R. 李远荣. (1998) *The memoirs of Lee Kong Chian.*《李光前传》 香港: 名流出版社. (Call no.: Chinese RSING 959.57 LYR-[HIS])
2. Nor-Afidah Abd Rahman and Wee, J. Lee Kong Chian, *Singapore Infopedia.* https://eresources.nlb.gov.sg/infopedia/articles/SIP_978_2006-06-16.html
3. Wikipedia. Lee Kong Chian. https://en.wikipedia.org/wiki/Lee_Kong_Chian
4. Chew, M. (1996). *Leaders of Singapore.* Singapore: Resource Press, p. 24. (Call no.: RSING 920.05957 CHE)
5. National University of Singapore. *Our chancellors: Speeches and biographical sketch (Lee Kong Chian).* http://www.lib.nus.edu.sg/nusbiodata/bioleekc.htm (Retrieved: 12 May 2016)

# 5 Banking

## Three Chinese Banks

In the early days, merchants who came to Singapore needed banks to handle the financial aspects of their trades. Initially, European banks dominated the banking industry. As the Chinese community grew in Singapore, the different dialect groups established their own banks. Hokkien businessmen went to Hokkien banks, and Cantonese businessmen went to Cantonese banks. The most successful bankers were Hokkiens, and three of their banks were most prominent: the Chinese Commercial Bank, the Ho Hong Bank, and the Oversea-Chinese Bank.

The oldest bank was the Chinese Commercial Bank (华商银行), which was started in 1912 by Lim Peng Siang (林秉祥), and he was soon joined by Dr. Lim Boon Keng. Five years later, in 1917, Lim Peng Siang started a second bank, the Ho Hong Bank (和丰银行). In 1931, Lee Kong Chian was invited to be the Vice-Chairman of the Chinese Commercial Bank.

After the First World War (1914–1918), the world economy grew rapidly, and there was incredible optimism. Industrialisation was expanding, and the stock market was booming. Everyone wanted to own stocks and were willing to buy on credit. Banks were willing to lend freely. Nobody expected the financial bubble to burst.

Lim Peng Siang (left) and Dr. Lim Boon Keng (right), who were both from the Chinese Commercial Bank.

## The Great Depression (1929–1939)

On 24 October 1929, the Dow Jones Industrial Index fell unexpectedly by 11%. The crash caused a chain reaction, and millions of people lost their entire life savings. The world economy went into a recession, and trade and businesses started to fail.

Singapore was also affected. In 1925, the price of rubber was $1.14 per pound, and in 1929, the price fell to 35 cents. In 1932, it plummeted to 6 cents per pound. Similarly, in 1925, the price of tin was $131.75 per picul but slipped to $104.32 in 1929 and fell further to $60.32 in 1931.

The rubber business had evaporated, and workers were laid off. Rubber plantation and processing factory owners who borrowed money could not repay their loans, and the majority of them were declared bankrupt. Even the ordinary man in the street was hit by a food crisis and could only afford rice and sweet potatoes.

Banks were affected. The British abandoned the gold standard and devalued the pound, causing banks that had made huge loans to bleed massively. Lee Kong Chian, who was recently appointed Vice-Chairman of the Chinese Commercial Bank in 1931, had to take immediate and drastic action. He was only 38 years old then, which was considered young to be tasked with the difficult problem of handling the impact of the global recession. He met with Ho Hong Bank's founding chairman, Lim Peng Siang, and they jointly agreed to merge their two banks. Upon hearing this merger, the managing director of the Oversea-Chinese Bank (华侨银行), Tan Ean Kiam (陈延谦), also wanted to join in.

Tan Ean Kiam

## Oversea-Chinese Banking Corporation (1932)

The three banks decided to merge and go into a partnership, with the objective of giving each other mutual support, so as to ride out the economic storm. They decided on the name Oversea-Chinese Banking Corporation (OCBC, 华侨银行), and this merged bank was established on 31 October 1932.[1]

It had an authorised capital of $40 million and a paid-up capital of $10 million, making it not only the strongest but also the largest local bank in Southeast Asia. It had a total of 17 branches in Singapore, Malaya, Indonesia (Dutch Indies), China and Hong Kong. The headquarters was located in the China Building at Chulia Street, Singapore.

Oversea-Chinese Banking Corporation, Chulia Street. It was demolished in 1970 to make way for the new OCBC building (see page 62).

Banking processes were streamlined to increase efficiency and thereby save money. The bank adopted the philosophy that it would place the interests of their clients as the highest priority.

The first joint managing directors of OCBC were Yap Geok Twee (叶玉堆, *Ye Yudui*) and Tan Ean Kiam. The chairman was Ho Hong Bank's co-founder, Chee Swee Cheng (徐垂青), and he served until 1936 when Yap Geok Twee took over. In 1938, Lee Kong Chian became chairman and he retained this position for 27 years until his retirement in 1964.

Right from the start in 1932, OCBC made a profit of $600,000. The chairman Chee Swee Cheng decided to place $500,000 into the bank's reserves, so as to give the bank a more solid and stable foundation that would act as a buffer to financial volatility. The remaining $100,000 would be used for projects, and this would give the bank more liquidity. This slow but steady approach for growing the bank was vindicated when the bank was able to pay shareholders their first dividends in 1937.

As the world's economy recovered from the Great Depression, OCBC benefitted tremendously. The price of rubber rose from a low of 6 cents per pound in 1932 to 20 cents per pound by the end of 1933. In the same period, the price of tin rose from £195 to £286 per metric ton. Then, in 1933, President Franklin D. Roosevelt introduced the "New Deal" economic policy in the United States, which helped Malaya's rubber export earnings to rise from $120 million in 1933 to $480 million in 1937. OCBC deposits increased from $34 million in 1934 to $57 million in 1940. Its reserves also rose to $13 million during this period.

However, OCBC faced many challenges resulting from the Great Depression. For example, they had loaned several companies, including Tan Kah Kee's Khiam Aik Company, huge sums of money that could not be repaid. Eventually Khiam Aik Company had to wind up, and Tan Kah Kee's business empire came to an end. Also, even though OCBC was considered a respectable size, but when compared to British banks like the Chartered Bank and the Hongkong and Shanghai Banking Corporation (HSBC) that held millions of dollars of deposits, it was considered a lightweight bank.

## Innovations

OCBC introduced innovative ways of doing things — it started a safe deposit box department and a hire purchase department. It also grew by starting new branches in Bangkok in 1934 and Kuala Lumpur in 1952. It became the sole agent for Postal Remittances and also for the Savings Bank of China, which enabled remittances to China.

Lee Kong Chian took over the chairmanship of OCBC from Chee Swee Cheng in 1938. He modernised the bank and introduced many reforms. One of the important changes Lee Kong Chian introduced was to have all the bank records kept in English. This helped in transactions with Europe and the United States. He also encouraged bilingualism among his bank staff, and he even produced a bilingual magazine, the *OCBC Echo*. To retain employees and increase the potential pool of talent, he introduced a bonus scheme.

## Philosophy of Corporate Governance

Lee Kong Chian introduced the philosophy of corporate governance. In the early days, loans were made to businessmen themselves or their friends without proper risk assessment. When a banker liked a particular client, deals were approved more readily. Even the appointment of professional managers tended to favour relatives and friends. Lee Kong Chian decided to implement a more objective assessment and to approve loans and appointments based on merit and not on favouritism.

## The Second World War (1939–1945)

On 1 September 1939, Hitler's Germany invaded Poland and started the Second World War. Actually, Japan had already invaded China, and the date that some historians use is of the Japanese invasion of Manchuria on 18 September 1931. They made further inroads by attacking Peking on 7 July 1937. China asked the overseas Chinese to help them fight the Japanese, and Lee Kong Chian's father-in-law, Tan Kah Kee, led the fund-raising to support China. Then on 7 December 1941, Japan attacked the United States in Pearl Harbor, which precipitated America's entry into the world war. The Japanese went on to invade Thailand and Malaya, and on 15 February 1942, Singapore fell to the Japanese.

Just two weeks before Singapore fell to the Japanese, a young 33-year-old Singaporean, Tan Chin Tuan (陈振传), was appointed joint managing director of OCBC, sharing the position with Tan Ean Kiam (unrelated), who was now 61 years old. The young Tan Chin Tuan was tasked to transfer the OCBC headquarters, assets and wealth to Chungking (重庆, *Chongqing*), China. He boarded a plane under the cover of night to fly to Batavia (now known as Jakarta), hoping to fly on to China. Unfortunately, all flights were cancelled, and so he took a Dutch river boat to Freemantle, Australia, and reunited with his family in Sydney. He took the opportunity to set up OCBC's first Australian branch during this time.

As Tan Chin Tuan's major objective was to set up a main branch of OCBC in Chungking, China, he decided to travel there via India. In the middle of 1943, he took a small British boat to Colombo, Ceylon (now Sri Lanka). This was a treacherous journey because there were Japanese submarines in this area, which later sank one of the three boats in the convoy. In September 1943, Tan Chin Tuan made his way to Calcutta, and then learnt that the wartime Kuomintang government in China had forced all banks in China to give up their assets to the government. He therefore decided not to continue to China, and instead set up an OCBC branch in Bombay (Mumbai), India.

In the meantime, the Japanese used the fifth floor of Fullerton Building as their office for the Japanese Inspector of Banks, and the Japanese State Bank office was located on the fourth floor of the Mercantile Bank Building. Non-Japanese were not allowed to use the lifts and had to take the stairs. This was a struggle for Tan Ean Kiam, who was in poor health, and just one year later, on 30 March 1943, he passed away due (it was claimed) to stress and humiliation, among other factors.

During the war, Lee Kong Chian was fortuitously attending a rubber association meeting in New York, and was unable to return to Singapore. Two of his sons and two daughters were already in America, and they remained in the United States until after the war.

The war ended when Nazi Germany surrendered on 8 May 1945, and after two atomic bombs were dropped on Hiroshima and Nagasaki. The Japanese surrendered on 5 September 1945.

Thus, OCBC survived a second crisis.

## Post-War Singapore

The war had killed some 70,000 Singaporeans, according to Lee Kuan Yew, Singapore's founding Prime Minister. People were living in terror, tortured and starved while homes and roads had been destroyed. The war had crippled Malaya and Singapore's economy by the razing of the rubber, palm oil and pineapple plantations; and associated factories were in ruins. Once the war ended, Lee Kong Chian flew back to Singapore with trepidation. To his sorrow, he found that the Japanese had totally devastated all his rubber factories and offices.

The British wanted to rebuild Singapore, and in order to do this, they needed to restore the local currency back into the banking system. They sought the help of all eight local banks, and on 17 September 1945, these banks were reopened for business. The British chose to start with OCBC because Lee Kong Chian maintained close ties with the British. They introduced a series of monetary and fiscal policies that guaranteed the channelling of money into banks for them to manage rehabilitation and reconstruction projects.

As the world economy was recovering, Singapore banks were doing well in the 1950s, and several new banks were set up, creating competition with each other. To gain an advantage, banks developed a new range of products and expanded their markets. Traditional Chinese banks began to do business with non-Chinese companies, including European and Indian companies. By 1947, OCBC made a profit of over $3 million, and it held a reserve fund of $2 million.

## Trade Unions

Despite the recovery of the economy after the war, the British could not address all the outstanding problems. Food was still scarce and rice had to be rationed; unemployment was still extensive, and wages did not increase. Strikes started to emerge. In October 1954, some 7,000 dockworkers went on strike, followed by hospital staff, firemen, and even cabaret girls.

In 1948, the communists of Malaya tried to force the British out, and they started armed struggles. On 31 August 1957, Tunku Abdul Rahman declared independence of Malaya from the British Empire. This independence sentiment spread to Singapore, and led by the People's Action Party, Singapore began demanding full self-governance in 1959.

Unions were formed in some banks, including the Chung Khiaw Bank (崇侨银行), OCBC, and the foreign bank First National City Bank of New York. The unions tended to be left-wing and they demanded higher wages for the lower-waged workers. In 1957, bank staff from these banks began to join in by taking an aggressive posture, threatening to go on strike if they did not receive higher wages. On 1 May 1958, an agreement was reached, and some bank staff received a pay rise, and retirement benefits were incorporated into their contracts.

However, three years later, in 1961, another battle arose when the unions demanded higher wages for non-clerical staff. Devan Nair was the union leader and led the fight against the banks. Later, he would become the President of Singapore. Initially, the unions rejected the bank's offer to settle the issue through an independent arbitration court, but later they agreed to send their case to the Industrial Arbitration Court, which ruled in favour of the unions. Unfortunately, the dispute continued, and the unions and bank quibbled over details of the award. More confrontation and threats arose, leading to a 13-day strike. Finally, Finance Minister Goh Keng Swee and Prime Minister Lee Kuan Yew came down on the side of the unions. OCBC followed the arbitration court rulings as interpreted by the unions, and they compensated the workers who had gone on strike. This helped repair relationships between management and the unions.

## Business Growth

By the 1950s, international trade routes were reopening, and the production of commodities, including rubber and tin, increased. The Korean War (1950–1953) caused further increased demand for rubber, so the price rose from 30 cents per pound just before the war started and shot up to $2.30 per pound during the war. The Malayan economy also expanded, and in 1955, their banks' earnings rose to $9.62 billion, which was more than $1.59 billion for the same period in 1954. In 1949, OCBC's bank assets were $164 million, and in just one year, in 1950, its assets increased to $220 million. OCBC introduced mobile banking in the 1950s and established more branches in Singapore.

The Oversea-Chinese Banking Corporation's first Singapore branch opened along South Bridge Road in 1938.

British businesses started to withdraw from Singapore during the 1950s, and OCBC took advantage of this by buying up several of their companies, including Fraser & Neave, Robinson and Co, Straits Trading, Great Eastern, and Raffles Hotel. This move helped convert OCBC from a mainly Chinese-business orientated bank into a conglomerate embracing the Singapore and the Malayan regional economies.

In 1964, OCBC started to rebuild their Chulia Street headquarters. The new OCBC Centre was designed by the America-Chinese architect I. M. Pei, and at that time, was the tallest building in Southeast Asia.

The new OCBC Centre at Chulia Street was opened in 1976 — it was designed by I. M. Pei. Photo by Terence Ong.

## Expulsion from Malaysia

On 9 August 1965, Singapore was separated from Malaysia after just under two years of joining. The fear was that Singapore would lose its Malaysian market, and it would be difficult to generate funds to survive. Already, there was a 10% unemployment rate as well as labour unrest. The problem was compounded by the British announcement in 1967 that they would withdraw their forces from Singapore, thereby leaving Singapore undefended. At that time, about 40,000 Singaporeans were working at the British base, and closing the military base would exacerbate the unemployment rate and income situation for these employees.[2]

To quickly generate income, the Singapore government tried hard and managed to attract large foreign companies to invest in Singapore. They included American companies such as National Semiconductor and Fairchild, followed by Texas Instruments, Hewlett-Packard and General Electric. Tax incentives for investments were quickly implemented, including tax exemptions and reliefs, such as up to a 90% remission of tax profits for approved enterprises for up to 15 years.

The Singapore government also built infrastructure to support industrialisation. It set up the Port of Singapore Authority to take over the function of the Singapore Harbour Board and to assume responsibility for the vacated British Naval Base, converting it into Sembawang Wharves. It established the Neptune Orient Lines to provide shipping services, and it modernised communication services such as postal, telegraph, telephone, and telex services. Education and training was improved. A National Wages Council was set up to enhance labour relationships and to reduce strikes and work stoppages.

This was a new era in Singapore's political and economic landscape, and banks had to rapidly adapt to the new master plan. They could no longer rely solely on financing individual merchants or trade in commodities. They had to diversity their customer base and look at a much wider world. They had to look at industrialisation and manufacturing, especially emerging new technologies.

OCBC adapted quickly and took advantage of the expansion of Singapore's economy. It already had branches in Johor Bahru (1962) and Ipoh (1964), and by 1966, it had 23 branches in West Malaysia. Then, in 1967, it decided to set up its first branch in London. OCBC was fortunate to employ a foreign exchange dealer familiar with the British system of obtaining licensing, and they managed to get much faster approval. In 1969, OCBC opened its London branch located in the heart of the British financial district, and this gave it additional credibility and trustworthiness. By 1971, OCBC had branches in many parts of the world, including Japan, the United States, and Russia.

In 1965, OCBC was described as a "nonentity" because hardly anyone knew of its existence in Singapore, that tiny red dot island barely visible on the world map. By the 1970s and beyond, OCBC helped transform Singapore into one of the most influential financial centres in Asia, and some say, the world.[3]

## Leadership Change

Lee Kong Chian had helmed OCBC from its beginnings in 1932. But, in 1964, his health deteriorated, and he was diagnosed with liver cancer. He stepped down as chairman of the bank in 1965. Lee Choon Seng (李俊承), one of the original founding directors of OCBC, took over his place. Then, in 1966, Lee Seng Wee, who was Lee Kong Chian's youngest son, aged 35 years then, took over his father's role as director of the bank. In 1967, Lee Choon Seng passed away at the age of 78. Tan Chin Tuan, who was the managing director of OCBC, was then appointed as chairman to take over from Lee Choon Seng.[4]

Lee Seng Wee (1930–2015)

Tan Chin Tuan (1908–2005)

## Development

Thanks to Lee Kong Chian, OCBC is a highly regarded multinational banking and financial services institution with its headquarters in Singapore. It is one of the larger banks in the Asia-Pacific region.

It currently has about 570 branches in 18 countries and regions, including all Southeast Asian countries, and it also has branches in China, Hong Kong, Macau, Korea, Japan, Australia, Dubai, the United States, and the United Kingdom. It has assets of more than $520 billion, and is considered one of the safest banks in the world.

## References

1. Low, A. (2017) *Wind Behind the Sails: The Story of the People and Ethos of OCBC*. Singapore: Straits Times Press. ISBN 9789814747639
2. Wikipedia. OCBC Bank. https://en.wikipedia.org/wiki/OCBC_Bank
3. History, SG. OCBC Bank. https://eresources.nlb.gov.sg/history/events/60688ba6-4e53-4945-9e48-9759eb4e01f0
4. Tan, E. Tan Chin Tuan. *Singapore Infopedia*. https://eresources.nlb.gov.sg/infopedia/articles/SIP_155_2004-12-27.html

# 6 Political Vision

## Introduction

Lee Kong Chian had witnessed how the corruption of the Qing Dynasty had traumatised society, and he had also lived under the hardship of Japanese militarism.

Lee Kong Chian was not only a businessman but also a person who cared about society, his country and the people. Never for a moment did he forget his motherland. If his home country was politically stable and the economy good, everyone would be happy; but if the motherland was not peaceful, he became deeply troubled. Thus, he believed that the happiness of a nation relied on a fundamental principle that rulers had to serve their people with a pure heart.

## The Kuomintang

Dr. Sun Yat Sen (1866–1925) met some revolutionary friends in Hong Kong in 1891. They were frustrated with the corrupt Manchu Qing Dynasty government, so together, they decided to lead a revolution to overthrow the government.

In 1912, when Lee Kong Chian was 19 years old and studying at the Tangshan College of Railway and Mining, he was a supporter of Sun Yat Sen. Unfortunately, the college was closed by Yuan Shikai. So Kong Chian could not continue his university education and had to return to Singapore in 1912.

A year later, in 1913, Sun Yat Sen started the Kuomintang party. Initially, both Lee Kong Chian and Tan Kah Kee supported Sun Yat Sen, and the latter raised money for him. But in 1918, Sun Yat Sen was joined by General Chiang Kai-shek, and both were anti-communists. Then, in 1927, Chiang Kai-shek carried out a purge of suspected Communists and dissidents in Shanghai, massacring thousands of people. When the Japanese invaded Manchuria, China, in 1931, the United States supported Chiang Kai-shek to fight the Japanese. But throughout the war, and even after it ended, Chiang Kai-shek continued to brutally treat the communists and their supporters. Both Tan Kah Kee and Lee Kong Chian were against unwarranted violence, and so they changed their stance.

## Nanyang Overseas Chinese Relief Association

On 7 July 1937, the Lugouqiao (Marco Polo Bridge) Incident (卢沟桥事变) broke out when a Japanese army commander demanded the right to search a town near Beijing to look for a missing Japanese soldier. The Chinese army was incensed by this order and started shooting at the Japanese. This incident is said to have been the start of the second Sino-Japanese War leading to the Second World War.

Emotions in China was already boiling from the Japanese capture of Manchuria, and people were denouncing the crimes of Japanese aggression. At that time, thousands of overseas Chinese were also inflamed, and they responded by lighting the torch and holding signs that read: "Resist the Japanese and save the country". Singaporean Chinese organised the "Nanyang Overseas Chinese Relief Association" and held a conference in Singapore, presided over by overseas Chinese leaders Tan Kah Kee and Li Zhendian (李振殿). Lee Kong Chian was also one of its effective members raising funds to support China's fight against the Japanese. He was the first to donate $300,000, the largest donation at that time.

In 1937, Lee Kong Chian became the chairman of the board of Nanyang Commercial Daily (*Nanyang Siang Pau*, 南洋商报), which was founded by Tan Kah Kee. The Chinese newspaper reported the war situation every day. It praised the patriotic Chinese and was anti-Japanese by revealing their atrocities, and it proclaimed that the salvation of China should be the goal of the overseas Chinese. Due to its large and wide circulation, this newspaper created a huge social impact in Singapore, Malaya and other Southeast Asian countries.[1]

In 1939, Lee Kong Chian became the first president of the Singapore Overseas Chinese Chamber of Commerce. Under his leadership, this most influential society of overseas Chinese had unprecedented unity, and cooperated with the "Nanyang Relief Association" in their anti-Japanese movement. Hence, it played an important role in raising relief funds, resisting the buying of Japanese goods, and organising teams for the resistance. After the fall of Singapore and Malaya, and during his stay in the United States, Kong Chian actively assisted the Allied forces to train military and political personnel and participated in the work of the International Red Cross and organised the Chinese in the United States to participate in anti-Japanese activities. Thus, despite being stuck in the United States throughout the war, Lee Kong Chian was able to strongly support the war of resistance against the Japanese occupation.

According to the financial authorities who controlled the funds for the Japanese resistance, monthly donations were more than $70 million, with the Nanyang Relief Association giving more than $20 million every month, accounting for almost one-third of the funds for the resistance. If the annual remittance from all the overseas Chinese given to the Nanyang Relief Association amounted to over $300 million, the Singapore contribution accounted for about half the total.

There were also more than 10,000 young Singaporeans who voluntarily returned to China to participate in the anti-Japanese war, most of them being skilled personnel. During the eight-year war of resistance, the overseas Chinese donated money and contributed manpower until the end of the war in 1945.

## Singapore Chinese Chamber of Commerce

After the Second World War, among the Chinese in Singapore and Malaya, Lee Kong Chian was one who cared about local politics. He identified with the country, and advocated eliminating factions so as to create not just a united Chinese society but a society that was inclusive of all other ethnic groups; and together they would join up and struggle for an independent democracy. History has, within half a century, proven that Lee Kong Chian's sober realistic ideas and practical actions were correct. His farsighted and broad vision had a positive and far-reaching impact on Chinese society in Singapore and Malaya.

As early as June 1945, when the Second World War had not quite ended, Lee Kong Chian published an article in *The Times* titled "Future Malaya", in which he advocated that the Chinese and Malays of Singapore and Malaya should join together to create a Malay federation. He quoted the research results of historians, saying: "The Chinese people have lived in Kelantan for 700 years, and tomb stones in Malacca have proven that the Chinese have also lived in Malacca since the 15th century. It is universally acknowledged that Chinese immigrants are law-abiding and diligent, they are peaceful, have no political ties, and no obligations to their former home country." Lee Kong Chian continued writing: "To say that Chinese immigrants have political or territorial ambitions here, is groundless." Malaya's development "came through the sweat and blood, the labour and lives of the Chinese people ... and actual harmony among the different ethnic peoples of Malaya has always been there".

He also recalled playing and reading with Malay children since young and working together with them when he grew up. He said that "Malaya [was] an opportunity for development in the economic arena and [would] benefit everyone". He advocated that the places where Malays lived, including the Dutch East Indies (Indonesia) and Borneo, could all form a greater federation of Malaya. He envisioned the formation of Malaysia nearly two decades before it finally materialised in 1963.

Shortly after the war, Lee Kong Chian was once again elected president of the Singapore Overseas Chinese Chamber of Commerce. He repeatedly appealed to the Chinese society saying: "I hope the overseas Chinese living in Southeast Asia will wholeheartedly participate in local construction work in the political, economic, educational and cultural arenas; we seek to further develop local undertakings and improve welfare for all." He also made it clear that "it is useless for us overseas Chinese who have left China, to talk about China's domestic politics because this will cause division and lower the status of the overseas Chinese". He advocated that the overseas Chinese should coexist with their neighbours of all ethnic groups and be benevolently close to all of them. He advocated carrying forward the thousands of years of Chinese cultural and moral values and the ethos of a Great Togetherness (大同).

## Opposing the Kuomintang

In 1946, Tan Kah Kee founded a new newspaper, the *Nanqiao Chinese Daily* (南侨日报), whose purpose was to oppose Chiang Kai-shek and the United States' support of him, and to welcome the new communist China. This had a great influence in the business community; the *Nanqiao Chinese Daily* was regarded as a "fortress of democracy" but at the same time, it was also considered socialist in its ideology.[2]

Soon after the Second World War, Tan Kah Kee wrote to President Harry Truman to ask the United States to stop all assistance to the Kuomintang government and withdraw their troops from China. At that time, it was not easy to raise share capital. Tan Kah Kee donated $110,000, and Lee Kong Chian donated $15,000 to the communists in China. All these actions by Tan Kah Kee deepened the friendship between him and China's communist party. Both Chairman Mao Zedong (毛泽东) and Premier Zhou Enlai (周恩来) had their inscriptions on the *Nanqiao Chinese Daily*. Later on, Tan Kah Kee moved to China, where he spent the rest of his life.

In 1947, when China's Kuomintang government asked the overseas Chinese to elect deputies and legislators to the National Congress, Lee Kong Chian immediately opposed it, believing that this measure was not appropriate. As the president of the Singapore Chinese Chamber of Commerce, he said that the Chinese living in Singapore and Malaya should not participate in the political activities in China. He believed that local citizens should wholeheartedly participate in local political, economic, educational and cultural activities to improve peoples' lives. These thoughts and remarks of Lee Kong Chian were consistent with the new communist Chinese government that was established in 1949. The policy of this new government supported the dual identity of overseas Chinese, separate from mainland China.

When the British colonial government decided shortly after the Second World War to form the Federation of Malaya, which forcibly separated Singapore and Malaya and simultaneously implemented restrictions upon overseas Chinese applying for citizenship and participation in politics, it was again opposed by Lee Kong Chian. He believed in having Singapore and Malaya under one government and that the overseas Chinese should be given citizenship together with all citizen rights, like all the other overseas nationalities. Singapore's *Nanqiao Chinese Daily* reported about this struggle led by Lee Kong Chian, believing that it was in line with the trends of the time.

## Dutch Colonialists

After the Japanese war, Dutch colonialists slaughtered overseas Chinese in Indonesia, seized and looted their ships, and blocked their trade. For this reason, the overseas Chinese community in Singapore raised a fierce struggle against the Netherlands. Lee Kong Chian was very sympathetic to the Indonesian Chinese and accompanied their leader, Zhang Chukun (张楚琨), to the shipping bureau of the British authorities to protest against the Dutch colonists and ask for the return of the looted goods. Lee Kong Chian spoke English very well and was good at mediating negotiations. In the end, the detained shipments were returned, and the Dutch colonial authorities apologised and compensated for the losses.

## Multiculturalism and Open-Mindedness

After the Second World War, the Chinese in many parts of Southeast Asia were subjected to restrictions including the deprivation of Chinese education and the use of the Chinese language, as against the promotion of the country's national language. Maintaining the survival of Chinese schools and striving for the legal status of the Chinese language and literature became one of the focuses of the political struggles of the Chinese. As early as 1946, Lee Kong Chian expressed his inclusive views on nationality and culture, citing that Switzerland succeeded in incorporating four languages: French, German, Italian, and Romansh.

Although Lee Kong Chian believed in maintaining Chinese cultural traditions and actively practised its moral teachings, he was educated in different schools, including an Anglo-Tamil School, where he learnt to speak English and Tamil. Then, when he did much of his rubber business in Malaya, he interacted with Malay, Indian and Chinese workers. Living in multicultural Singapore also helped to give him a multicultural and multilinguistic understanding of society.[3,4]

Lee Kong Chian practised and tried diligently to realise his political thoughts that "all ethnic groups should move forward hand in hand". He ran charitable public welfare projects and treated the Chinese, Malays, Indians, and other races equally. When Singapore and Malaysia advocated learning Malay, he was already 70 years old; yet he still listened to the radio in Malay, hired Malay teachers, and studied tirelessly to improve his Malay. In 1967, when he learned that he was elected as the 34th honorary president of the Chinese General Chamber of Commerce, he resolutely resigned, and asked the Chamber of Commerce to amend the constitution, firmly abolishing factions. He said: "Today we are all Singaporeans. Why do we still have regional concepts and why divide each other?" Lee Kong Chian's political vision and words and deeds have made outstanding contributions to Singapore's multicultural society. His philosophy of embracing different ethnic groups, religions, languages and political systems showed his tolerance and open-mindedness.

His political beliefs acknowledged that there are advantages to the free enterprise approach to the economy and that the communists, too, have a point in sharing the nation's wealth. Lee Kong Chian's middle-of-the-road approach is his all-embracing liberal socialist political vision.

Portrait of Lee Kong Chian.

## References

1. Suryadinata, L. (editor) (2010). *Tan Kah Kee and Lee Kong Chian in the Making of Modern Singapore and Malaya*. Singapore: National Library Board. ISBN: 139789810853501
2. Yong, K.-F. (1986). «Nanyang Chinese Patriotism towards China knows no political Boundaries»: The Case of Tan Kah Kee (1874–1961). *Archipel* **32**: 163–181. https://www.persee.fr/doc/arch_0044-8613_1986_num_32_1_2317
3. *Guanghua Daily* 光华日报, 23 February 1948.
4. Seah, L. (2015). Jinan University, Lee Kong Chian and the Nanyang Connection 1900–1942. *BiblioAsia*. https://biblioasia.nlb.gov.sg/files/pdf/vol-4/issue-1/v4-issue1_JinanUniversity.pdf

# 7 A Humanitarian

## Introduction

Lee Kong Chian came from a poor family background, but he went on to become one of the wealthiest persons in the world. He was conferred many titles and was appointed chairman of numerous societies. Yet he maintained humility and lived a simple and frugal lifestyle; he possessed absolute integrity and was friendly and caring to his colleagues and workers; he was passionate in supporting education; he generously donated a large portion of his wealth to educational and charitable institutions, and he changed countless lives. Many countries, including Singapore, Malaysia and China, benefitted from his altruism.[1,2]

## Supporting Education

Lee Kong Chian was totally dedicated to education. The late Prime Minister of Singapore, Lee Kuan Yew, described Lee Kong Chian as "a respected member of the community not just because he amassed a great wealth but more because of the contributions he made to the advancement of our society, particularly in the field of education".

In his 1962 convocation address to graduates of the University of Singapore, he advised the new graduating students: "Seek truth relentlessly and state it fearlessly, always keeping in mind that you must seek the truth through the methods of reason and not through your emotion."

Lee Kong Chian believed in offering his time and leadership abilities to help others. His interest in social and philanthropic work started early. In 1918, when he was 25 years old, he was a member of the management

Statue of Lee Kong Chian in front of the Kong Chian Administration Centre, Hwa Chong Institution.

committee of Chinese High School (华侨中学, now known as Hwa Chong Institution), which had been founded by his father-in-law, Tan Kah Kee.[3]

Lee Kong Chian was devoted to supporting education and had forward-thinking ideas. He believed that education not only imbued human wisdom, but also helped the development of knowledge and culture. These would guide and enable a country to become economically rich and strong.

In 1927, the year he got married, he donated money to Xiamen University (厦门大学). In 1938, he founded the Kuo Chuan Primary School (国专小学)

Lee Kong Chian at the flag-raising ceremony marking the founding of the University of Singapore, 1962.

in his hometown of Furong, China, and in 1943, he started the Kuo Chuan Secondary School (国专中学), also in Furong. The school name he chose was to honour his late father, Lee Kuo Chuan (李国专).

Lee Kong Chian's generosity was all-inclusive and not restricted by ethnicity, culture or religion. He was one of the first Chinese businessmen to introduce scholarships for Malay students in 1951, and he donated to the Islamic College in Klang (Kolej Islam Sultan Alam Shah), Malaysia. He also donated funds to build the Umar Pulavar Tamil School, the only Tamil-medium high school in Singapore.

Meeting University of Singapore students in 1964.

As part of his interest in education, in 1953, he donated $375,000 towards the construction of the new Raffles National Library (renamed the National Library) at Stamford Road, and stipulated that the fund be given on condition that this new library be free and public.

Lee Kong Chian also gave his time to help many causes. From 1934 to 1955, he was the chairman of Chinese High School (Hwa Chong Institution). In 1949, he donated money to the school to build a science block, a sports field, a teachers' hostel, and the Kuo Chuan Library, named after his father. Lee Kong Chian also helped introduce bilingual education in the school.

In 1953, he proposed a nationwide bilingual and trilingual education, and this was accepted and incorporated into the colonial government's education policy. The following year, there were student protests from Chinese schools against the British's proposal for national service, and he was personally involved in negotiations between the government and students.

Lee Kong Chian laying the foundation of Raffles National Library (National Library) in 1957.

During the Malayan Emergency of 1948–1960, when insurgents tried to overthrow the colonial British government, Lee Kong Chian stood up for Malayan rights. This was misinterpreted by the British, who perceived him to be pro-communist. Similarly, the Chinese felt he was too westernised, and the Malayans felt he was too Chinese-oriented. In fact, Lee Kong Chian was pushing for an independent Malayan-cum-Southeast Asian identity and self-rule.

Lee Kong Chian was the first Asian Chancellor of the University of Singapore (1962–1965). In his installation address, he quoted the ancient Chinese philosopher Mencius saying: "It gives real delight to be able to gather from around us the most talented individuals, so as to teach and nourish them." He realised that bolstering education is an important means towards economic, social and character development. He firmly believed that the education of the young generation was an important responsibility and formidable ambition that he was willing to personally and conscientiously carry out throughout his life. He travelled around

Lee Kong Chian meeting students of Chinese High School (Hwa Chong Institution), 1956.

Western Europe in March 1962 to study foreign education and bring home new ideas. His social public welfare charities were also focused on the promotion of education. Some 75% of his donations were used for education, although this gradually fell to 50% after 1974, when the Singapore government established more schools and the population profile changed.

Lee Kong Chian believed in traditional Chinese culture and moral values, so he contributed money to establish many Chinese schools to fulfil the potential talents of thousands of primary school to university students in both Singapore and Malaya. The Lee Foundation he created spared no effort to sponsor poor students who had good results but faced difficulties paying their school fees and needed urgent help.[4–6]

## Xiamen University and Jimei Schools

Lee Kong Chian was not only committed to the development of education and social welfare in Singapore and Malaysia, he also loved his home country, where his father and brother were staying. After the closing of his father-in-law Tan Kah Kee's company in 1934, he continued to provide annual fundings for Xiamen University and the Jimei Schools in Fujian, China.

Jimei School, Fujian.

When the Kuomintang bombed Xiamen University around 1946, he donated a large amount of money to repair the university building, which had been badly damaged. He helped build the university auditorium, the new Chengyi Building, swimming pools, gymnasiums, and more than ten buildings.

Xiamen University

Statue of Lee Kong Chian with Tan Ai Leh at Xiamen University Medical College. Photo from: https://inf.news/en/world/ffcac0b7898f2a8f9f895ca9f4898ff8.html

In his hometown of Meishan, Furong village, he donated a large sum of money to establish the Kuo Chuan Kindergarten, the Kuo Chuan Primary School (which has four campuses), the Kuo Chuan Middle School, and the Kuo Chuan Hospital, all named after his father.

## Other Activities

During his lifetime, Lee Kong Chian held many positions in educational institutions, several organisations and community service societies. He was the Chancellor of the University of Singapore and the Chairman of the Chinese High School (which now includes Hwa Chong Institution and Hwa Chong International). He was also the President of the Chinese Chamber of Commerce & Industry. Overseas organisations that he was involved in included being the President of the Royal Commonwealth Societies, President of Great Britain-China Centre, President of the Federation of Commonwealth Chambers of Commerce, and President of Britain Burma Society. For community service, Lee Kong Chian was the first chairman of the Singapore Council of Social Service in 1961.

## The Lee Foundation

李氏基金

LEE FOUNDATION

Lee Foundation

Even before he started the Lee Foundation, Lee Kong Chian had already established a charity fund in 1930 that he called the Lee Kuo Chuan Grant, named after his father. Twenty-two years later, in 1952, he started the Lee Foundation, and he donated $3.5 million of his own money taken from his shares of the Nanyi Rubber Group. This has been an important charity that has helped an incalculable number of people, as well as societies and institutions.

Having started as one of the first private charitable foundations in Singapore, the Lee Foundation has become a leader in philanthropy, with hundreds of millions of dollars funding a wide array of causes and institutions with no conditions attached.

Through the Lee Foundation and the Lee family, Lee Kong Chian was involved in many enterprises and formed a huge network for these enterprises. He became one of the most successful Chinese entrepreneurs in Singapore and Malaya. By the end of the 1960s, the total area of his rubber plantation had reached 12 million square metres, and there were as many as 35 affiliated institutions of Nanyi Rubber Company. In addition to traditional rubber and pineapples, it also operated 25 companies in mining, transportation, shipping, timber, food, publishing, banking, and insurance.

Small donations from the Lee Foundation were arranged according to protocol, and the amount of funds could vary, depending on the business situation, which affected the annual investment dividend income. Hence, the amount given out depended upon the income of that year. Large and special contributions to the Lee Foundation came from the annual instalments of annual accounts from Singapore, Malaysia and Hong Kong. Each year, profits from the shares of the Nanyi Group went to the Lee Foundation.

For more than 70 years, the Lee Foundation donated generously to a wide range of causes, including the expansion of schools, hospitals, homes for the elderly and disabled, cultural institutions, disaster relief, and also for helping individual poor students. As long as the person or institution met the purpose and guidelines of the Lee Foundation, the donation would be given, regardless of ethnic origin, religious belief, regional affiliation, or any other conditions. Its sponsorship range remains very wide, spread throughout Singapore, Malaysia and around the world.

In 1960, the Lee Foundation was divided into two divisions, each established separately in Singapore and Malaysia. Then, in 1965, the Lee Foundation established a branch in Hong Kong to take care of charitable needs for that region. Six directors managed the fund.

In Singapore, donations included $150 million to Nanyang Technological University's new medical school, $60 million to the new National Reference Library at Victoria Street, a $50-million donation to the Singapore Management University, $25 million to the Natural History Museum at the National University of Singapore, and many other institutions and societies. The Lee Foundation is often the first place those who need funds go to, and it receives over 100 requests and appeal letters daily.

The Lee Foundation has made great and far-reaching contributions to education, social development, and the advance of civilisation. The spirit of this fund is epitomised in the saying: "Get from society, use for society".

Lee Seng Gee

Lee Seng Tee

Lee Kong Chian's philanthropic spirit continued even after his death. When he died in 1967, he left half of his fortune to the Lee Foundation, so that it could continue his charitable work. His eldest son, Lee Seng Gee, took over the management of the Lee Foundation until Seng Gee passed on in 2016. Then, the second son, Lee Seng Tee, managed the foundation from 2017 until 2022, when he passed on too.

The educational institutions, libraries, hospitals, old peoples' homes, special schools, temples, churches, etc., helped by Lee Kong Chian and the Lee Foundation, are listed in the Appendix.

## Personal Involvement

In 1958, the Welfare Association was established in Singapore, and Lee Kong Chian was appointed its president, and he continued until 1964. During his tenure, he helped in relieving poverty and also in disaster relief. This included a fire at the Tiong Bahru vegetable garden's four-foot pavilion, and the floods in Toa Payoh and Potong Pasir. He would personally visit the disaster areas, talk to the victims and their relatives, and inspect the amount of damage. The Lee Foundation was always the first to donate significantly in disaster relief. Lee Kong Chian would also request for further donations from the public to help victims through their difficulties.

Shortly after he was appointed the first Chairman of the Singapore Council of Social Service (now the National Council of Social Service), a raging inferno (now known as the Bukit Ho Swee fire of 1961) erupted that destroyed the homes of 16,000 kampong dwellers. Senior Civil Servant Goh Sin Tub spotted Lee Kong Chian queuing up to donate funds to help relief efforts. When the former asked the latter to follow him to the office, Lee Kong Chian said that it did not feel right jumping the queue.

A former Council member also recalled: "What marked the Council from the early days was the type of leadership provided by the late Dato Lee Kong Chian. He was humble, energetic and always at the field of action."

Tan Kay Hai, one of the former presidents of the Singapore Swimming Association, recounted that when he needed support for this association, he approached Lee Kong Chian. He was invited to his office where Lee Kong Chian opened his money drawer, asked how much was needed, and then immediately handed over the amount.

It was not just money he donated. He also believed in donating blood, which he did 18 times in his life, once just before his birthday celebration dinner. He explained the reason why he donated blood was because it was something that only a person could give, especially when there was a shortage of it in the Singapore blood bank.

Lee Kong Chian was well known for his humility and humanity. Malcolm MacDonald, the former Commissioner-General for the United Kingdom in Southeast Asia said: "Dato Lee has remained utterly unspoilt, humble and unassuming in spite of the extraordinary influence that he can exercise in commerce, finance and politics. His humanity is one of the marks of his true greatness."

## Awards

Lee Kong Chian received many awards for his humanitarian and philanthropic works. He was conferred the honorary degree of Doctor of Laws by the University of Malaya in 1958. In his acceptance speech, he highlighted the importance of cultural exchange. He stated that the education facilities in Singapore and Malaya were second to none in Southeast Asia and geographically, both countries were in the transportation hub between East and West, something they should take advantage of. In 1965, in recognition of his services to the University of Singapore and his contributions to arts and education, he was accorded the honorary degree of Doctor of Letters.

Lee Kong Chian, Chancellor University of Singapore, 1962.

Lee Kong Chian was installed as Chancellor of the University of Singapore in 1962 but resigned in 1965 due to ill health.

In 1964, Malaysia's Yang di-Pertuan Agong (head of state), Putra of Perlis, awarded Lee Kong Chian the title Panglima Mangku Negara (PMN); hence, Kong Chian was known by the honorific *Tan Sri*. Prior to that, Kong Chian had been made a Dato' by the Sultans of Johor and Kelantan in 1957 and 1959, respectively.

The Lee Foundation contributed to several universities, Chinese middle schools and Chinese primary schools in Singapore and Malaysia. Donations were given to the Universiti Malaya, Nanyang Technological University, the National University of Singapore, Ngee Ann Polytechnic, Kolej and Universiti Tunku Abdul Rahman (Malaysia), and others.

In addition, the Lee Foundation contributed generously to help medical institutions, including the Negeri Sembilan Chinese Maternity Hospital, the Medical Centre, and the Chinese Medical Aid Department. The Lee Foundation also provided academic scholarships and grants to students from low-income families and helped those students to complete their studies when they faced financial problems. Money was given to these students regardless of their gender, race, religion, place of origin or geographical location, as long as the applicants had excellent academic performance and fulfilled the requirements.

The Lee Foundation was the unanimous choice for the Special Recognition Award at the Inaugural National Volunteerism and Philanthropy Awards in 2004 and received the Presidential Medallion for Social Philanthropy in 2011. These and countless other recognition awards are a fitting legacy for Lee Kong Chian, a true Singapore folk hero.

## Illness

Lee Kong Chian's health deteriorated in 1964. He had been diagnosed with liver cancer by Dr. Seah Cheng Siang in January 1964, who referred him to Queen Mary Hospital in Hong Kong, where the diagnosis was confirmed. He was operated upon on 18 January 1964. His Hong Kong oncologist suggested he go to Shanghai for further treatment with Chinese herbal medicines. While he was in Shanghai, he was invited to Beijing to meet Prime Minister Zhou Enlai (周恩来), and they talked for 15 minutes.

Lee Kong Chian being met by Zhou Enlai during a visit to China in 1964.

Lee Kong Chian meeting Zhou Enlai in China, 1964.

He returned to Singapore three months later, where his health initially improved. However, his liver cancer progressed unremittingly, and two years later, his condition took a turn for the worse, and he passed away peacefully on 2 June 1967 at his mansion at Mount Rosie. His funeral service was held at Mount Vernon Crematorium, and many people from all walks of life came to pay their last respects. At that time, Lee was survived by his wife, three sons, three daughters and several grandchildren.

Paying respects at the wake of Lee Kong Chian, June 1967.

Despite the great wealth he amassed, Lee Kong Chian remained humble and gracious throughout his years. Even on his death bed, he requested that his funeral be kept simple. Journalists who covered his funeral described it as "devoid of grandiose display" — "The fire lit by Lee Kong Chian would not extinguish, but would be passed down generation to generation".

## References


1. Nor-Afidah Abd Rahman and Wee, J. Lee Kong Chian, *Singapore Infopedia*. https://eresources.nlb.gov.sg/infopedia/articles/SIP_978_2006-06-16.html
2. Wikipedia. Lee Kong Chian. https://en.wikipedia.org/wiki/Lee_Kong_Chian
3. Suryadinata, L. (editor) (2010). *Tan Kah Kee and Lee Kong Chian in the Making of Modern Singapore and Malaya*. Singapore: National Library Board. ISBN: 139789810853501
4. Chew, M. (1996). *Leaders of Singapore*. Singapore: Resource Press, p. 24. (Call no.: RSING 920.05957 CHE)
5. Li, Y. R. 李远荣. (1998) *The Memoirs of Lee Kong Chian*.《李光前传》 香港: 名流出版社. (Call no.: Chinese RSING 959.57 LYR-[HIS])
6. Visscher, S. (2007) *The Business of Politics and Ethnicity: A History of the Singapore Chinese Chamber of Commerce and Industry*. Singapore: NUS Press, p. 48. (Call no.: RSING 381.0605957 VIS)

# 8 Legacy

## Introduction

Lee Kong Chian and his Lee Foundation have left such an enormous legacy that it would be virtually impossible to describe all the contributions in one book. Therefore, only major accomplishments and benefactions that have made the greatest impact on society and individuals are included here. Many of his involvements in companies, associations, societies, institutions, and with people from several countries will unfortunately be left out. You can view the list of places and institutions named after Lee Kong Chian or his father, Lee Kuo Chuan, in the Appendix.

Lee Kong Chian established Lee Rubber Company and was a co-founder of the Oversea-Chinese Banking Corporation, and three of his innovations were adopted by the Singapore government — the equivalent of the Central Provident Fund (CPF), the concept of housing loans, and variable annual bonuses for workers depending on the profits achieved that year. He proposed bilingual education, which was also accepted by the Singapore government. He was President of the Chinese Chamber of Commerce & Industry, Chairman of Hwa Chong Institution (previously known as Chinese High School), and the first Chancellor of the University of Singapore. Holding these and other high positions enabled him to introduce original ideas that improved the functions of these institutions. For example, he wanted education to be more rounded to uphold the principles of integrity and altruism. He also believed that students should learn through hands-on practical experiments and experiences. Indeed, he was far ahead of his times.

The following are the more prominent legacies of Lee Kong Chian and his Lee Foundation that are still making an impact today.

## Lee Kong Chian School of Medicine

Lee Kong Chian School of Medicine

The Lee Kong Chian School of Medicine (LKCMedicine) was started as a joint medical school between Nanyang Technological University (NTU) and Imperial College London. It is Singapore's third medical school, and it received $150 million from the Lee Foundation. The school was established with the aim of training a new generation of doctors who will not only be competent in clinical skills but also equipped with a strong foundation in research and innovation.

The history of LKCMedicine can be traced back to 2010 when Singapore's Ministry of Education announced plans to establish a third medical school in collaboration with a renowned international partner. In 2011, NTU signed an agreement with Imperial College London, one of the world's leading institutions in medical education and research, to jointly establish LKCMedicine.

The medical school is divided into a preclinical campus in the Yunnan region in the west of Singapore (where NTU is located) and a clinical campus in the Novena area of central Singapore, where Tan Tock Seng Hospital is located.

Medical students of the Lee Kong Chian Medical School making a physician's pledge at the white coat ceremony.

The school opened its doors in August 2013, admitting its inaugural batch of students. LKCMedicine offers a five-year undergraduate medical program, known as the Bachelor of Medicine and Bachelor of Surgery (MBBS) program, which incorporates a unique curriculum that emphasises team-based learning (TBL) and early clinical exposure. The TBL approach used at LKCMedicine encourages students to actively engage in their learning by working through real-world clinical cases in small groups. This method helps develop critical thinking and problem-solving skills while integrating basic sciences with clinical medicine. Students also have early clinical exposure from their first year, providing them with hands-on experience in healthcare settings.

Team-based learning for Lee Kong Chian Medical School students.

LKCMedicine's curriculum is designed to produce doctors who will not only be skilled clinicians but also adept at research and innovation. Students are exposed to research opportunities from the start of their training, with the aim of fostering a culture of inquiry and discovery. The school actively promotes interdisciplinary research collaborations and encourages students to undertake research projects alongside their clinical studies.

Medical students entertaining fellow students.

The students themselves are very active in organising community service, which include public health projects, helping migrant workers, enhancing awareness and working with special needs individuals, and visiting palliative care centres and homes of the elderly.

In addition to its educational programs, LKCMedicine is committed to advancing medical research and innovation. The school has established research centres and institutes focused on various areas, including cardiovascular and metabolic diseases, infectious diseases, neuroscience and mental health, caring for an ageing population, and global health problems. These research initiatives contribute to Singapore's healthcare ecosystem and help address important medical challenges, both locally and globally. Intersecting with these programmes are cross-cutting themes such as data science, artificial intelligence, developmental biology, and regenerative medicine and microbiome medicine. LKCMedicine explores synergies among its different research projects as well as across different disciplines.

The number of students admitted is currently around 150. In addition to the usual A-level or International Baccalaureate, students have to take another British exam, followed by a series of interviews. The students participate in community services that help the elderly and disadvantaged, both in Singapore as well as overseas. Graduates either practise general medicine or continue into a specialty. The school also gives out Lee Kong Chian Medical Scholarships for selected medical students for the full five years of their course, and the scholarship is unbonded.

Despite being such a young medical school, LKCMedicine has quickly gained international recognition for its innovative curriculum, research contributions, and commitment to medical education. It has rapidly risen in the worldwide as well as Asian rankings for medical schools.

## References


1. Lee Kong Chian School of Medicine (2015) *Making of a Medical School: Lee Kong Chian School of Medicine*. Singapore: Nanyang Technological University. ISBN: 9789810959807
2. Nanyang Technological University. Lee Kong Chian School of Medicine. https://www.ntu.edu.sg/medicine
3. Wikipedia. Lee Kong Chian School of Medicine. https://en.wikipedia.org/wiki/Lee_Kong_Chian_School_of_Medicine

## Lee Kong Chian Reference Library

Lee Kong Chian Reference Library at Victoria Street.

The National Library of Singapore and the Lee Kong Chian Reference Library are two important institutions in the history of Singapore's library system.

### *National Library of Singapore*

The National Library of Singapore traces its origins back to 1823 when a private subscription library called the Singapore Library was established by Sir Stamford Raffles, the founder of modern Singapore. Over the years, the library went through several transformations and relocations. In 1953, the government decided to establish a new national library. Lee Kong Chian donated $375,000 towards the building of the National Library at Stamford Road, and it was opened in 1960. However, due to rapid urban development, a larger and more modern building was needed.

The original National Library of Singapore at Stamford Road.

## *Lee Kong Chian Reference Library, Victoria Street*

The new Lee Kong Chian Reference Library at Victoria Street.

In 2005, the new 16-storey National Library Building located at Victoria Street was erected. It received a donation of $60 million from the Lee Foundation, and was named the Lee Kong Chian Reference Library. The Reference Library is a branch of the National Library Board of Singapore, and specialises in reference materials. The library houses a vast collection of books, periodicals, newspapers, and other materials, serving as a repository of Singapore's published heritage. It also offers a range of services, including research facilities, exhibitions, and educational programs.

It was designed by the ecologically conscious architect Ken Yeang; the building has many environment-friendly architectural features, and has received many tributes both at home and abroad.

Inside the new Lee Kong Chian Reference Library at Victoria Street.

The Reference Library was opened in 2005 and is designed to cater to researchers, scholars and students who require access to a wide range of reference materials. It offers an extensive collection of books, periodicals, maps and multimedia resources, with a focus on subjects like history, social sciences, literature, humanities, science and technology. The Reference Library provides specialised services and facilities for in-depth research, including dedicated reference librarians and study areas. It also has a specialised collection on Singapore and Southeast Asia, which includes rare books and manuscripts.

Over the years, the Lee Kong Chian Reference Library has expanded its services and resources, including the development of a digital collection and online resources. It also organises exhibitions, talks and workshops to promote lifelong learning. Both the National Library of Singapore and the Lee Kong Chian Reference Library played or are playing crucial roles in preserving Singapore's cultural heritage, supporting education and research, and promoting a love for reading and learning among the public.

Today, the Lee Kong Chian Reference Library continues to be an important institution in Singapore's intellectual landscape, providing access to a wealth of knowledge and resources to support the nation's development and growth.

## References


1. Yong, C. Y. National Library Building (Victoria Street). *Singapore Infopedia.* https://eresources.nlb.gov.sg/infopedia/articles/SIP_1834_2011-08-31.html
2. Heirwin Md Nasir. National Reference Library. *Singapore Infopedia.* https://eresources.nlb.gov.sg/infopedia/articles/SIP_935_2005-01-24.html
3. Wikipedia. National Library, Singapore. https://en.wikipedia.org/wiki/National_Library,_Singapore
4. National Library Board. About the Lee Kong Chian Reference Library. https://reference.nlb.gov.sg/about-us/lkcrl/


## Lee Kong Chian Natural History Museum

The Lee Kong Chian Natural History Museum.

Dinosaur skeletons.

The Lee Kong Chian Natural History Museum, named after its major benefactor, is the most prominent natural history museum in Singapore. The museum houses over 560,000 specimens and artefacts related to natural history, including plants, animals, fossils, and minerals from Southeast

Asia and other parts of the world. The specimens are used for education, research, and public outreach programmes.

The origins of the Lee Kong Chian Natural History Museum can be traced back to the establishment of the Raffles Museum in 1874. The Raffles Museum was initially set up to house a small collection of zoological and botanical specimens gathered by the Singapore National Academy of Sciences and the Asiatic Society of Singapore. Over the years, the museum's collection grew steadily, with contributions from various researchers, scientists and collectors.

It was renamed the Natural History Museum of Singapore in 1965, and its collection continued to expand. However, due to limited space and the need for better facilities, plans were made to establish a new and larger natural history museum. In 1972, the Raffles Museum was relocated to a new building within the National University of Singapore (NUS) campus at Kent Ridge.

In 2007, Lee Kong Chian's Lee Foundation offered to donate $25 million to NUS for the construction of a new natural history biodiversity museum. This donation was a significant milestone in the development of the museum and led to the renaming of the museum as the Lee Kong Chian Natural History Museum in his honour.

The construction of the new seven-story museum began in 2011 and was completed in 2014. The Lee Kong Chian Natural History Museum opened to the public in 2015. Its popular attractions include three large dinosaur skeletons in the main exhibition hall. Other highlights include a vast array of animal specimens, including the skeleton of a whale, numerous mammals, birds, reptiles, and insects, as well as botanical specimens and geological artifacts.

Inside the Lee Kong Chian Natural History Museum.

The Natural History Museum's exhibits include the Biodiversity Gallery, which showcases the diversity of life in Southeast Asia, and the Heritage Gallery, which features the history of the Museum and the work of early naturalists in Singapore. The Museum also has a Learning Lab, where visitors can participate in hands-on activities and workshops.

In addition to its public outreach programs, the Lee Kong Chian Natural History Museum is also involved in research on biodiversity and conservation in Southeast Asia. The museum's scientists work on a wide range of topics, including the discovery of new species, the study of ecosystem dynamics, and the development of conservation strategies.

It offers various educational programs, exhibitions and workshops for students, researchers, and the general public. The museum also actively collaborates with international institutions and participates in biodiversity conservation efforts in the region.

The Lee Kong Chian Natural History Museum has become a popular destination for Singaporeans and tourists alike, providing a unique opportunity to explore and appreciate the rich natural heritage of Southeast Asia and beyond. It continues to play a vital role in promoting awareness and understanding of the natural world and its conservation. Overall, the Natural History Museum is an important institution for the study and conservation of biodiversity in Southeast Asia, and it serves as a valuable resource for researchers, educators, and the general public.

## References

Tan, K. Y. L. (2016) *Of Whales and Dinosaurs: The Story of Singapore's Natural History Museum*. Singapore: NUS Press. ISBN: 9789814722131.

Chua, A. Lee Kong Chian Natural History Museum. *Singapore Infopedia*. https://eresources.nlb.gov.sg/infopedia/articles/SIP_1689_2010-07-15.html

Wikipedia. Lee Kong Chian Natural History Museum. https://en.wikipedia.org/wiki/Lee_Kong_Chian_Natural_History_Museum

## Hwa Chong Institution

Hwa Chong Institution at Bukit Timah.

Hwa Chong Institution (HCI), formerly known as Chinese High School, is a prestigious independent school in Singapore known for its academic excellence and holistic education. The institution has had notable contributions by two prominent philanthropists, Tan Kah Kee and Lee Kong Chian. Tan Kah Kee founded the Chinese High School in 1919 to cater to the needs of primary school leavers of the Chinese community in the region. He was the father-in-law of Lee Kong Chian, who was invited to be the chairman of the school board, which he served from 1934 to 1955.

Lee Kong Chian made many donations to HCI that were named in honour of his late father, Lee Kuo Chuan.

Kuo Chuan Auditorium, Hwa Chong Institution.

## *Kuo Chuan Auditorium*

This auditorium is a key venue for school assemblies, concerts, plays, and other performances. It provides a platform for students to showcase their talents and express themselves artistically.

Kuo Chuan Centennial Art Gallery, Hwa Chong Institution.

## *Kuo Chuan Centennial Art Gallery*

The Kuo Chuan Centennial Art Gallery received donations from the Lee Foundation, and was officially opened in 2020 on the 100th anniversary of the school. The Gallery now houses the works of Singapore's pioneer artists, such as Liu Kang, Cheong Soo Pieng, Chen Wen Hsi and Chen Chong Swee, who were former HCI teachers. The Gallery also features artwork by established alumni artists, thus exhibiting HCI's distinctive artistic heritage.

A bust of Lee Kong Chian in the Kong Chian Library, Hwa Chong Institution.

## *Kong Chian Library*

Lee Kong Chian donated money for the library, and he named it the Kuo Chuan Library. However, when he passed away in 1967, the school renamed it the Kong Chian Library in honour of Lee Kong Chian.

## *Lee Kong Chian Lecture Theatre*

Lee Kong Chian donated funds to construct the Lee Kong Chian Lecture Theatre, a state-of-the-art facility within HCI's campus. This lecture theatre serves as a venue for various academic and cultural events, including lectures, performances and competitions.

Statue of Lee Kong Chian outside the Kong Chian Administration Centre.

## *The Kong Chian Administration Centre*

The main administration building of HCI is named the Kong Chian Administration Centre. It is an office for the administrative staff and the principals of HCI. Many important awards that HCI won over the years are exhibited on the second floor of this building.

The contributions of Lee Kong Chian and the Lee Foundation have greatly enhanced the educational experience at HCI, providing students with state-of-the-art facilities, research opportunities, and financial support to excel in their academic and personal development. HCI has, over the years, been highly ranked among Singapore schools.

## References

1. Wikipedia. Hwa Chong Institution. https://en.wikipedia.org/wiki/Hwa_Chong_Institution

2. Hwa Chong Institution. (2019) *Hwa Chong Centennnial Commemorative Book.* Singapore: Hwa Chong Institution. https://www.hcalumni.sg/hwa-chong-centennial-commemorative-book/
3. Hwa Chong Institution. Hwa Chong Institution Prospectus. https://static1.squarespace.com/static/606a6979b5fef3342d8dd877/t/60c96adfe5610a39ef167c45/1623812842505/Hwa+Chong+IP+Prospectus+Latest.pdf

## Lee Kong Chian School of Business, SMU

Lee Kong Chian School of Business, Singapore Management University.

The Lee Kong Chian School of Business (LKCSB) is the business school of the Singapore Management University (SMU). It opened in 2000, and it focuses on areas of business, economics and management. It also promotes academic research with economic and industrial relevance. The campus moved three times and its present campus is along Bras Basah Road, close to the business and financial centre of Singapore.

In 2004, the Lee Foundation contributed S$50 million to SMU, and the Singapore government matched the grant to create a world-class business school. Its syllabus follows that of the Wharton School of Business,

University of Pennsylvania, and it has continued to introduce innovative learning programs.

Students attending a lecture at the Lee Kong Chian School of Business.

The LKCSB pioneered a collaborative learning environment known as the SMU-X, which explores experiential learning. This educational programme employs first-hand, real-world experience through projects, internships, and partnerships with industry affiliates. It is also committed to research, and its faculty members are currently engaging in research across various disciplines and the results published in international academic journals.

Students are encouraged to have a global perspective through international exchange programs and study trips. They are given the opportunity to immerse themselves into different cultures, learn about international business practices, and build a global network.

LKCSB is a dynamic Asian business school with over 400 full-time faculty staff and 9,000 undergratuate and 3,000 postgraduate students. Its graduates have contributed to Singapore's business landscape and beyond. Despite being a relatively young business school, LKCSB has gained international recognition and accreditation, and the School has consistently been ranked among the top business schools in the world.

## References


1. Sim, C. Singapore Management University. *Singapore Infopedia.* https://eresources.nlb.gov.sg/infopedia/articles/SIP_500_2005-01-19.html
2. Wikipedia. Singapore Management University. https://en.wikipedia.org/wiki/Singapore_Management_University
3. Lee Kong Chian School of Business SMU website: https://business.smu.edu.sg/
4. Singapore Management University, https://www.smu.edu.sg/about/facts


## Lee Kong Chian Gardens School, MINDS

Lee Kong Chian Garden School, Movement for the Intellectually Disabled of Singapore (MINDS).

The Lee Kong Chian Gardens School is an educational initiative that caters to individuals with intellectual disabilities in Singapore. It is part of the Movement for the Intellectually Disabled of Singapore (MINDS), which manages several schools whose aims are to provide quality education, vocational training, and support for individuals with intellectual disabilities as well as their caregivers.

In 1961, a group of concerned parents and professionals met to address the lack of educational opportunities for children with intellectual disabilities in Singapore, and they started a pilot project in Towner Road with one class of students and teachers. The following year, in 1962, they formed the Singapore Association for Retarded Children (SARC), which was renamed the Movement for the Intellectually Disabled of Singapore (MINDS) in 1985. This group also started other schools and a residential home in Tampines. The school that was set up at Margaret Drive in 1969 became the headquarters of MINDS. All the schools had the name "Gardens School" attached to them to reflect the idea of nurturing and cultivating the potential of these children. In 1984, the school at Margaret Drive was renamed the Lee Kong Chian Gardens School, in recognition of a generous donation from the Lee Foundation.

Individuals attending the MINDS school.
Photo credit: MINDS

Over the years, the Lee Kong Chian Gardens School expanded its operations and services to meet the growing needs of the intellectually disabled community in Singapore. This includes vocational training and employment support for adults with intellectual disabilities, and it plays a key role in promoting public awareness and understanding of the issues faced by these individuals and their families.

Painting a paper lantern.
Photo credit: MINDS

Learning taiko drumming at the MINDS school.
Photo credit: MINDS

Today, MINDS continues to evolve, with a growing emphasis on promoting inclusion and empowering individuals with intellectual disabilities to lead meaningful and fulfilling lives. The Lee Kong Chian Gardens School remains at the forefront of this movement, providing holistic education that includes art, music, physical exercises, and social and vocational training, as well as employment support to individuals with intellectual disabilities.

Learning how to prepare food for cooking.
Photo credit: MINDS

The Lee Kong Chian Gardens School has played a crucial role in empowering individuals with intellectual disabilities to become more independent. It also advocates for their rights and inclusion in society, which it does in collaboration with the government, private corporations, and the community. Thus it continues to make significant contributions to the education and well-being of this community in Singapore.

## References

Lee Kong Chian Gardens School. https://www.minds.org.sg/for-children/schools/lgs/

Lee Kong Chian Gardens School. https://www.roots.gov.sg/en/places/places-landing/Places/landmarks/my-queenstown-heritage-trail/lee-kong-chian-garden-school

Cherian, M. (2002). *Many Dawns*. Movement for the Intellectually Disabled of Singapore.

Tan, E.S. (2012). *A Special Journey*. Movement for the Intellectually Disabled of Singapore.

# 9 Down Memory Lane

## Lee Kong Chian Photos

Portrait of Lee Kong Chian (date unknown).

Lee Kong Chian with his wife Ai Leh and four children, taken in the USA during the 2nd World War.

Sketch of Lee Kong Chian, 1946.

Goh Loo Club 40th anniversary in 1949: front row 4th from far right Lee Kong Chian, 7th from right Lim Boon Keng, 8th from right Tan Lark Sye.

Lee Kong Chian on the telephone, 1952.

Lee Kong Chian front row 10th from right at groundbreaking ceremony of Nanyang University, 1955.

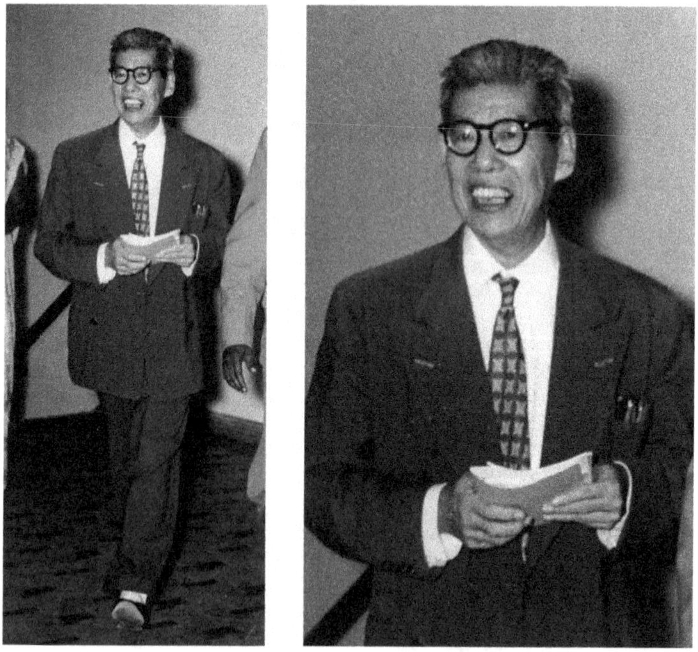

Lee Kong Chian, photos taken when attending his eldest daughter Lee Seok Keng's wedding in London, 1953.

Lee Kong Chian on the left sitting with Tan Lark Sye on the right during the opening ceremony of Nanyang University, 1958.

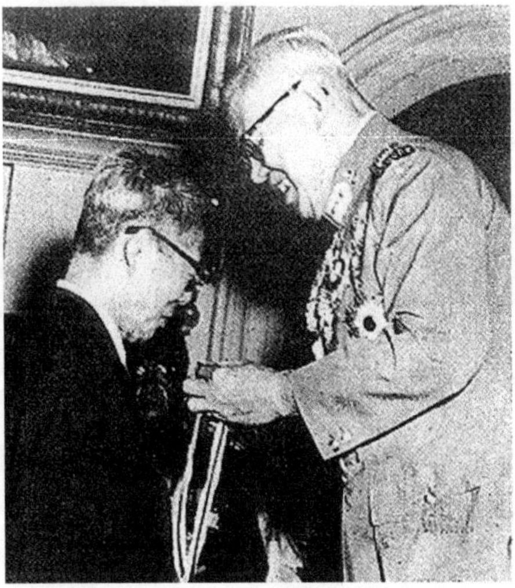

Lee Kong Chian conferred Datuk by the Sultan of Kelantan, 1957.

Lee Kong Chian conferred First Class Datuk by the Sultan of Johore, 1959.

Lee Kong Chian, Chairman of the Singapore Welfare Association (standing), 1958.

Lee Kong Chian, 2nd from right, accepting a cheque from the Chinese Chamber of Commerce on behalf of the Singapore Welfare Association, 1959.

Lee Kong Chian with his wife Ai Leh at the Singapore Welfare Association carnival, 1960.

Lee Kong Chian, standing, with Ko Teck Kam president of the Chinese Chamber of Commerce on the left, 1960.

Lee Kong Chian with Ko Teck Kam, president of the Chinese Chamber of Commerce, on the left, and Tan Lark Sye of Nanyang University in a white shirt on the right, 1960s.

Lee Kong Chian, president of the Chinese Swimming Association, with swimmer Neo Chwee Kok who is receiving an award from Governor-General Franklin Gimson 1950s.

Lee Kong Chian at Hwa Chong Institution, seated 5th from the left, 1960s.

Lee Kong Chian photo in the ZaoBao newspaper (year unknown).

Lee Kong Chian, Chairman of OCBC Bank (standing), at the opening ceremony of the Penang Land Building 1960s.

Lee Kong Chian portrait painting at the Academy of Medicine Singapore.

Lee Kong Chian cutting the ribbon at the Liu Kang exhibitn at Victoria Memorial Hall, 1962.

Laying the Foundation of the Iron Steel Mill by Lee Kong Chian (standing on the left), 1962.

Lee Kong Chian, Chancellor of Singapore University, 1962.

Lee Kong Chian, Chancellor of Singapore University visiting the UK, 1962.

Lee Kong Chian in China, 1965.

Lee Kong Chian and Wang JinSheng at the Kaiyuan Temple Quanzhou, China, 1965.

Lee Kong Chian sketch portrait (date unknown).

Lee Kong Chian unveiling his bronze statue, Xiamen University, 2013.

Lee Kong Chian's bronze statue in China.

# Final Words

Lee Kong Chian is one of the most important and inspirational personalities in the history of Singapore and Southeast Asia. His entrepreneurial spirit enabled him to set up and manage several highly successful companies, and he helped establish and run the Oversea-Chinese Banking Corporation. He followed his mentor and father-in-law, Tan Kah Kee, in the philosophy of giving back to society which was exemplified by both their philanthropy. They were also ardent defenders of the Chinese language and culture. Throughout the decades, Lee Kong Chian and the Lee Foundation, which he set up, has supported individual students from disadvantaged backgrounds and made generous donations to numerous educational institutions. His emphasis on education is captured in an analogy he used for his inaugural speech as Chancellor of the University of Singapore: "Whoever wants to harvest good rice, must also plant good seeds." Lee Kong Chian has changed the history of Singapore and his legacy continues to benefit countless students who, in turn, have improved the lives of many others.

In the final analysis, it is Lee Kong Chian's integrity, humility, frugal lifestyle, generous philanthropy, and selfless desire to help others that will be the beacon of light for everyone to follow. The whole of humanity has benefitted from his altruism. This is his ultimate legacy, and his name will always be remembered.

Lee Kong Chian

# Appendix

## Titles Conferred, Places Named After Lee Kong Chian

Lee Kong Chian Chancellor of the University of Singapore

Tan Sri Lee Kong Chian garnered multiple honours for his contributions to the society. He was conferred the Honorary Doctor of Laws in 1958 by the University of Malaya, Singapore, and the Honorary Doctor of Letter in 1965 by the University of Singapore.

In 1964, he received the Panglima Mangku Negara, which carries the honorific title "Tan Sri". He received the Seri Paduka Mahkota Johor in 1957 and the Seri Jiwa Mahkota Kelantan in 1959.

## Positions Held in Schools, Centres and Societies

During his lifetime, Tan Sri Lee Kong Chian held numerous positions in schools, centres and societies. He was the President of the Royal Commonwealth Societies, President of Great Britain-China Centre, President of the Federation of Commonwealth Chambers of Commerce, President of the Britain-Burma Society, and President of the Chinese Chamber of Commerce & Industry. In addition, he was also Chairman of the Chinese High School (now known as Hwa Chong International).

## Major Contributions and Awards

**1924:** Becomes a member of the management committee of Singapore Chinese Girls' School.

**1934:** Takes over Tan Kah Kee's biscuit factory, agreeing to donate one-third of its annual profits to Xiamen University and the Jimei Schools in China. He also rents out his rubber mills in Singapore, with an understanding that Kong Chian would allocate 20% of their annual profits to these educational institutions.

**1934–1955:** Serves as chairman of the management committee of the Chinese High School. In 1949, he convinces the principal to introduce bilingual education. He also builds a science block, a sports field, a teachers' hostel and the Kuo Chuan Library (named after his father), among his other gifts for the school.

**1938:** Founds Kuo Chuan Primary School in his home town of Furong, China.

**1939–1940:** Serves as president of the Singapore Chinese Chamber of Commerce (SCCC).

**1943:** Founds Kuo Chuan Secondary School in Furong.

**1946–1947:** Serves as president of the SCCC and as a member of the Singapore Advisory Council.

**1949:** Starts two clinics at Kuo Chuan Secondary School. Donates $250,000 to the University of Malaya Endowment Fund over two years (instead of the planned 15 years); donates an additional $250,000 in 1951 for the acquisition of library resources and the promotion of Oriental studies and science.

**1951:** Sets up Nan'an Guozhuan Private Hospital (now known as Quanzhou City Guozhuan Hospital) in Furong.

**1951–1952:** Serves as chairman of Thong Chai Medical Institution, a free hospital in Singapore, and plans the purchase of land for the hospital's permanent building.

**1952:** Establishes the Lee Foundation with a capital sum of $3.5 million, with the aim of supporting cultural, educational, charitable and public organisations.

**1953:** Represents the SCCC and Chinese schools to seek increased government aid and clarification on the new bilingual policy to be implemented in Chinese schools; donates $375,000 to the construction of a National Library, on the condition that it would be a free and public library; pledges to match 10% of the total funds raised by the public for the setting up of Nanyang University.

The public fundraising effort raises $10 million by 1957 and he donates $1 million. He also donates $300,000 to the founding of Kong Hwa School.

**1954:** Mediates between the colonial government and protestors from Chinese schools during the student demonstrations against the National Service Ordinance.

**1955:** Donates to the Islamic College in Klang, Malaysia.

**1957:** Conferred the title of Datuk Paduka Mahkota Johore by the Sultan of Johor; donates 75% of the total building cost of Umar Pulavar Tamil School in Singapore.

**1958–1964:** Becomes chairman of Singapore Council of Social Services (now National Council of Social Services).

**1958:** Conferred the honorary degree of Doctor of Laws by the University of Malaya.

**1959:** Conferred the title of Datuk Sri Paduka Mahkota Kelantan by the Kelantan Sultan; donates to the Needham Research Institute in England, a centre for the study of East Asian science, technology and medicine.

**1961:** Donates $25,000 to help the victims of the Bukit Ho Swee fire. He previously donated to help the victims of many other *kampong* (village) fires that occurred during the late 1950s and early 1960s.

**1962–1965:** Serves as the first chancellor of the University of Singapore.

Lee Kong Chian Chancellor of the University of Singapore

**1962:** Donates $1 million towards the setting up of a medical college in the University of Singapore.

**1963:** Donates RMB$1,200,000 to help the Huaqiao (Overseas Chinese) University in China to build the Tan Kah Kee Memorial Hall.

**1964:** Conferred the title of Panglima Mangku Negara (Commander of the Order of the Defender of the Realm) by the head of state of

Malaysia; donates $200,000 towards the building of the Singapore Council of Social Services headquarters.

**1965:** Donates $1 million to the Singapore Medical Progress Fund for the setting up of the Institute of Medical Specialties at Singapore General Hospital; conferred the honorary degree of Doctor of Letters by the University of Singapore in recognition of his services to the university and his contributions to arts and education.

## Legacy

In 1953, Lee Kong Chian donated $375,000 for the construction of the National Library at Stamford Road on the condition that the library waived its annual fees and become a free public library. On 16 August 1957, Lee Kong Chian officiated over the laying of the foundation stone. In 2003, 50 years after this first donation, the Lee Foundation donated another $60 million to the National Library. To honour the contribution, the reference library at Victoria Street was named the Lee Kong Chian Reference Library. Continuing Lee's strong support for higher education, the Lee Foundation contributed $50 million to the Singapore Management University (SMU) in 2004. In recognition of this, SMU named its School of Business, the building, and its university-wide scholarship programme after Lee Kong Chian.

In 2011, the Lee Foundation donated $150 million to Nanyang Technological University's (NTU) new medical school. NTU's president, Professor Bertil Andersson, noted that this was the largest donation for academia locally. The Lee Foundation also contributed $25 million towards the construction of the Lee Kong Chian Natural History Museum at the National University of Singapore, which houses three dinosaur skeletons and over a million specimens from Southeast Asia.

## Places Named after Lee Kong Chian

- Lee Kong Chian Reference Library, National Library, Singapore
- Lee Kong Chian Wing, University Hall, National University of Singapore
- Lee Kong Chian Natural History Museum, National University of Singapore
- Lee Kong Chian Centre for Mathematical Research, National University of Singapore

- Lee Kong Chian School of Medicine, Nanyang Technological University
- Lee Kong Chian Lecture Theatre, Nanyang Technological University
- Lee Kong Chian School of Business, Singapore Management University
- Lee Kong Chian Faculty of Engineering and Science, Universiti Tunku Abdul Rahman
- Tan Sri Lee Kong Chian Hall, Methodist College Kuala Lumpur
- Lee Kong Chian Gardens School, LGS-MINDS
- Lee Kong Chian Library, Anglican High School
- Lee Kong Chian Auditorium, Anglo-Chinese School (Barker Road)
- Kong Chian Administration Centre, Hwa Chong Institution
- Kong Chen Hall, Chong Hwa Independent High School, Kuala Lumpur
- Kong Chian Hall, SJK (C) Cheng Siu 1
- Kong Chian Hall, Kuala Lumpur Selangor Chinese Assembly Hall
- Kong Chien Hall, Foon Yew High School, Johor Bahru
- Kong Chian Hall, Singapore [Chung Cheng High School (Main), Singapore
- Kong Chian Hall, Nan Chiau High School
- Kong Chian Library, Hwa Chong Institution (High School Section)

## Places named after Lee Kong Chian's Father

There are also a number of places named after Lee's father, Lee Kuo Chuan, including:

- Kuo Chuan Avenue, a road in Singapore's Marine Parade district
- Kuo Chuan Presbyterian Secondary School
- Kuo Chuan Presbyterian Primary School
- Heritage Centre, Hwa Chong Institution (High School Section), previously known as Kuo Chuan Centennial Arts Centre
- Lee Kuo Chuan Stadium, Anglican High School
- SRJK (C) Kuo Kuang (国光国民型华文小学) No. 1 and SRJK (C) Kuo Kuang No. 2 — Two Chinese medium primary schools in Skudai, Johor Bahru, Malaysia, named after Lee Kuo Chuan's and Lee Kong (Kuang) Chian's middle names.

# Honours

## *Honours of Malaysia*

- Malaysia :
  - Commander of the Order of the Defender of the Realm (PMN) — **Tan Sri** (1964)
- Kelantan :
  - Knight Grand Commander of the Order of the Life of the Crown of Kelantan (SJMK) — **Dato'** (1959)
- Johor :
  - Knight Grand Commander of the Order of the Crown of Johor (SPMJ) — **Dato'** (1960)

# Reference

1. Nor-Afidah Abd Rahman and Wee, J. Lee Kong Chian, *Singapore Infopedia*. https://eresources.nlb.gov.sg/infopedia/articles/SIP_978_2006-06-16.html

# Index

Printed in the USA
CPSIA information can be obtained
at www.ICGtesting.com
LVHW011110160824
788390LV00002B/6

9 789811 285219